The Cultivation of Roses in Pots
Or; Growing Roses in Containers

by William Paul, F.R.H.S.

with an introduction by Roger Chambers

This work contains material that was originally published in 1866.

This publication is within the Public Domain.

This edition is reprinted for educational purposes
and in accordance with all applicable Federal Laws.

Introduction Copyright 2018 by Roger Chambers

Self Reliance Books

Get more historic titles on animal and stock breeding, gardening and old fashioned skills by visiting us at:

http://selfreliancebooks.blogspot.com/

Introduction

I am pleased to present yet another title on Gardening.

The work is in the Public Domain and is re-printed here in accordance with Federal Laws.

As with all reprinted books of this age that are intended to perfectly reproduce the original edition, considerable pains and effort had to be undertaken to correct fading and sometimes outright damage to existing proofs of this title. At times, this task is quite monumental, requiring an almost total "rebuilding" of some pages from digital proofs of multiple copies. Despite this, imperfections still sometimes exist in the final proof and may detract from the visual appearance of the text.

I hope you enjoy reading this book as much as I enjoyed making it available to readers again.

Roger Chambers

PREFACE TO THE FIRST EDITION.

The Rose has long been a favourite flower, not only in England, but throughout Europe generally; and there is, perhaps, none other that has ever received such unlimited attention. The ardour manifested of late years in the cultivation of this flower has produced rapid improvements. Many varieties, which, for years past, have been held in high estimation, are now falling aside before the constant introduction of new varieties, which have materially widened the range of this beautiful genus, as well as improved the individual varieties of which it is composed. It is not, however, the design here to treat of Roses generally,* but of their cultivation in Pots; and this in as brief a manner as the explication of the subject will allow.

This system of cultivation has created some stir among lovers of Roses; and from the decided superiority of the specimens exhibited at the various horticultural exhibitions during the present year over those of the preceding, it would appear that Roses *are well adapted for Pot-plants*, and are likely to engage the attention of numerous plant cultivators.

The author would just remark that the following observations have been noted down at different times as they have occurred to him, and often somewhat hastily; and in sending forth this pamphlet he does not pretend to instruct his professional brethren, but merely to furnish what he considers *a desideratum* to those private amateurs who may wish for more particular information.

* "The Rose Garden," (second edition,) recently published, embraces the whole routine of culture.

PREFACE TO THE SECOND EDITION.

A THOUSAND copies of this little work having been sold in a brief period, the author's present object has been to convert the former hasty notes into more solid matter, and to add such information as he may have gained by observation and experience. As the first sale more than answered his expectations, he has, in the present edition, inserted a few wood-cuts, illustrative of the more difficult practices of Rose-culture; and thus, while the matter is considerably increased, the price remains as heretofore.

Paul's Nurseries, Waltham Cross, N.

OBSERVATIONS
ON THE
CULTIVATION OF ROSES IN POTS.

PRELIMINARY REMARKS.

THE idea of cultivating Roses in Pots as exhibition plants emanated from the Horticultural Society of London, which first offered prizes for the best specimens that should be produced. The offer did not meet with so ready a response as might have been expected. The exhibitor of flowers merely was not prepared all at once to incur the additional labour of producing the plants in pots. Besides, was it certain that they would succeed under this mode of culture? It was at best but an experiment; and hence, probably, the tardiness of some, and the total rejection of the scheme by others. But it is no longer necessary to speculate on the apititude of Roses for Pot-culture; their suitableness is now fully proved; and it rather appears remarkable that their capabilities should not have been earlier tested. While our floral exhibitions had their Heaths, Pelargoniums, and Fuchsias in pots, the blossoms only of the Rose were shewn; and these, jolted by travelling from a distance, or languishing from the heat of the exhibition tents, conveyed a very inadequate idea of the characters of a flower, whose chief beauty consists in its freshness. That the Rose, while easy of culture in a pot, requires great care and judgment *to bring to perfection by a given day*, cannot be denied; but this fact should have been no drawback to its *general* cultivation. This affects the *exhibitor only*, and affects every exhibitor alike.

Then, in regard to its worth of this special attention, we may say, that for beauty, variety, and sweetness, it yields to no other flower. The lengthened period for which it blooms, and the accommodating character of the plant—the various forms it is capable of taking—the differing soils in which it may be grown—are also points which lend to it an additional interest.

ADVANTAGES OF GROWING ROSES IN POTS.

One great advantage of growing Roses in pots is, that they may be removed from place to place at pleasure when in bloom. Another advantage is, that by this system plants may be had in flower throughout the year. Three sets of plants are requisite to accomplish this. The first, which are grown out of doors, or in a cold pit, will flower from May till November; the second, which are *retarded*, will flower from November till February; and the third set, which are *forced*, from February till June. To this point we shall shortly recur.

But there are other advantages, when plants are grown in pots, of which we are not able to avail ourselves when they are growing in the open ground. With regard to the *tender* varieties of Roses, these are very great, if we only take into consideration the facilities afforded of protecting them from frost and heavy rains, by means of pits or a house; and it is not surprising to find they thrive so much better under glass than when exposed to all the changes and severities of the weather. The hardy kinds, however, (except a few be introduced, by way of varying the colours to a greater degree,) certainly need not to be grown under glass: the pots should be plunged in the ground, and an airy, yet sheltered situation in the garden should be chosen.

SUGGESTION FOR GROWING TEA ROSES NEAR LONDON.

Hitherto the Chinese and Tea-scented Roses have not been grown with much success in the immediate neighbourhood of London, nor in the north of England, when planted in the open ground. It is notorious that no collection, however small, can be complete without some portion of these Roses; and it is the vexatious disappointment alone, attendant upon their constant failure, that could have caused their growth in certain localities to have been given up. Doubtless, in some instances, an impure atmosphere may have caused their failing; but it is my conviction that, if carefully examined, the soil and situation would more often explain the difficulty.

The ease, then, with which we can remedy these disadvantages, when the plants are grown in pots, leads me to propose their cultivation in this way to those with whom they have not hitherto succeeded; and there is good ground to believe they will succeed well in this manner, and especially if grown under glass. Except for forcing, cold pits are perhaps as good as a house; but wherever they may be placed, they should be kept close to the glass, and exposed to a free circulation of air. They should have the advantage of dews and soft showers; the lights in summer being merely used to protect them from cold nights or rough weather, and, by help of mats or canvas, from a hot sun.

METHODS OF GROWTH.

Among Roses there are two distinct kinds of plants:—worked plants, comprising the budded and grafted ones; and such as are grown on their own roots. Both succeed well in pots, but individual kinds often thrive better the one way than the other; and, in making a selection, it will be well to ascertain the mode in which each flourishes best. It has been said that a part of the plants should be grown to bloom in the natural season—from May till November; another part, as forced Roses, blooming from February to June; and the remainder, as retarded Roses, to enliven us with their brilliant tints and fragrance throughout the dreary months of winter. To secure flowers in the natural season will first engage our attention: forcing and retarding will be a matter for after consideration.

TRANSPLANTING AND POTTING.

Early in autumn, immediately after rain, is the most favourable time to remove both worked plants and others from the ground; and such as have grown moderately, with well-ripened wood, should be chosen. The sized pots best suited are 6 inch, 8 inch, 9 inch, and 11 inch, according to the size of the plant, and they should be well-drained. In potting, the soil should be pressed firmly in the pots, watering freely afterwards, through a fine rose, to settle the soil about their roots. So far of worked plants. The cultivation of the Autumnals on their own roots may be commenced at any season, as they are usually kept growing in pots. If purchased in spring, in 4-inch pots, they may be immediately shifted into 6-inch pots, then plunged and watered continually, as required. *Our aim being to get the plants strong, they should not be suffered to flower the first year.* We should endeavour, through the growing season, to bring them to form a few vigorous shoots, in preference to a greater number of weak ones. To accomplish this, it is advisable to rub out some of the buds when pushing, keeping in view the handsome formation of the plant. The plants may be shifted once or twice during the growing season, as required; and in the following spring we shall probably find them in 9-inch pots preparing for a vigorous growth and bloom.

THINNING OUT.

When potting, all suckers and soft wood should be cut out from the worked plants, and straggling shoots shortened back to within a few eyes. Where too thick, some of the shoots may be cut out entirely; from three to seven, in a young plant, according to the habit of growth, being, in most cases, sufficient. Thinning in summer, immediately after flowering, is very beneficial. The best ripened shoots should be left, and such as stand in the best position for the well-forming of the plant. The permanent shoots may be shortened in November and March; some at both periods: the former to obtain an early, and the latter a late bloom.

SOIL.

The soil in which Roses succeed well, and that generally used here, is, two parts of stiff turfy loam, broken up, but not sifted, two parts manure, (road gatherings laid by for a season, or the remains of a hot-bed, not too far decomposed,) and one part burnt earth or sand. This compost should be thrown up in a heap in autumn, and turned two or three times during winter, and a little newly-slaked lime scattered throughout, to destroy worms and grubs.

This is the soil used for the mass; but for the delicate varieties (Chinese, &c.) it may be improved by the addition of one part leaf mould, or well-pulverised manure.

PROTECTION.

After potting, the plants taken from the ground should be removed to a cold pit, syringing and shading, if sunny weather, for a week or ten days. Here they will soon form fresh fibrous roots, and scarcely suffer from their removal. It will be well if all the tender varieties can be allowed to remain in a pit during winter; otherwise they should be removed to the north side of a wall or fence, and a thatch of fern, or beech boughs, with the leaves on, formed; or any other mode of protection that can be more readily devised, to secure them from rain and frost. Indeed, it is clearly evident that the rains of autumn as seriously injure the delicate-rooted Roses as the frost in winter; for during the mild winter of 1842-43, many of these died, which was doubtless owing to their receiving too much moisture in autumn, whereby the roots perished. No plants require much water when in a comparatively dormant state.

Thus, then, the tender varieties may be protected from injury during winter, and the hardy ones may be removed from the pits about a month after being potted, and plunged at once in the open ground where intended to be grown and flowered.

PRUNING.

About the middle of November pruning may be performed, in order to effect an early bloom. The plants having been thinned out previously, all that is now required is, the shortening-in of the remaining shoots. It is a difficult matter to lay down any precise rules with regard to pruning, upon the judicious adaptation of which depends not only the well-forming of the plant, but, in a great measure, the perfection of bloom also. In order to prune Roses with certainty of success, we ought to know the character of each plant we are about to operate on; for Roses of the same group ofttimes require very different pruning. The best criterion we can offer is, perhaps, habit of growth. Among the Hybrid Chinese, the two favourite old Roses, Charles Lawson and Chénédolé, both vigorous growers, frequently occasion great disappointment by not blooming. The failure will probably be found to arise, in most cases, from the method of pruning. *These Roses, and others of like habit, should be well thinned out, and the shoots that are left for flowering shortened but little.* Others of the same group (Hybrid Chinese), that are weak or moderate growers, may be shortened-in close; such is Compte Lacépède, a beautiful and well-known rose. Then there are varieties of intermediate growth, which may be pruned in proportion. The groups Provence and Moss, may be pruned closer than the Hybrid Chinese. The Autumnal Roses there is little fear of pruning out of bloom; early or late, they are sure to flower. The Chinese and Tea-scented, when grown on their own roots, should be cut close, to induce them to throw up suckers from beneath the ground, as these will grow much stronger than shoots formed above ground, and flower beautifully through the summer and autumn. One point, too, should be borne in mind, that Roses, when grown in pots, may be pruned closer than when grown in the open garden. One season I shortened back the shoots of the newly-potted Autumnals, Gallicas, and Provence, from two to four eyes; and what with thinning and shortening, the plants looked very naked, and at first sight appeared to many to have been cut too much. But when considering that each of the remaining shoots would produce two, three, or four, and that the plants were not in the open ground, but in pots, it was evident such was not the case; and this their after growth and flowering fully confirmed. When dealing with the most vigorous kinds of Hybrid Chinese and Hybrid Perpetual, I left no more than six eyes on a shoot; and though the plants were young, and consequently small, their blooming, both as regards the size and the abundance of flowers, was all that could be wished.

REMOVAL OF TENDER VARIETIES.

By the end of March, if room cannot be granted them in pits, or a green-house, the tender varieties may be brought from their winter quarters, and plunged in an airy situation out of doors. Such as were left unpruned for late flowering should now be pruned. It should, however, be borne in mind, that if the plants can be allowed to remain in the pits through the spring they will bloom much earlier, in greater perfection, and the foliage will be of increased beauty.

PLUNGING.

It is an excellent plan, in plunging, to place the pots so that the bottoms rest on an inverted seed-pan or flower-pot. This secures a free drainage, prevents the roots growing through the bottom of the pot into the soil, and is an effectual barrier to the ingress of worms.

The pots may be plunged level with the ground, and so far apart that the plants may not touch each other when full grown. After plunging, it is beneficial to cover the surface lightly with decomposed hot-bed manure. It is the practice with some to set the pots on the level ground, filling up the interstices nearly to the rim with saw-dust or cinder-ashes: this in wet situations is the most preferable practice, but we do not approve of leaving the sides of the pots exposed fully to the air.

WATERING.

Water should be given abundantly *through the growing and blooming* season. Guano-water is an excellent manure for Roses in pots: it should, however, be used cautiously—an ounce to a gallon of water is sufficient. If, from the nature of the soil, or the state of the weather, the plants require watering oftener than once a week, pure water should be given at the intervening periods.

DESTRUCTION OF CATERPILLARS, GREEN FLY, &c.

When the buds first break, and continually afterwards, the plants should be keenly sought over, to destroy the grub and caterpillar, which travel from shoot to shoot, eating out the growing points, and thereby destroying the bloom. Some of these are mere threads in appearance, and can scarcely be detected till some mischief is done. A finely-pointed knife or a large needle is the best instrument for this purpose. The green fly is often very annoying. The most effectual way of ridding ourselves of these pests appears to be by removing the plants to a green-house, for the time, or enclosing them, as they stand in the beds, with a covering of wet garden-mats placed double, or oiled canvas, and then fumigating with tobacco.

DISBUDDING, &c.

When the buds first push, if two or three break close together, the weakest, or those taking the least favourable direction, should be rubbed out. Such shoots as are inclined to grow rank, without blooming, should be stopped, or taken out if not wanted to form the head, for they appropriate to themselves the sap which should be directed into the flower-branches; and, further, render the plants of uneven growth. Any flower-buds which are forming imperfectly should be nipped out; and the size of the first flowers may be increased, by removing, at an early stage, the small backward flower-buds.

SUCKERS.

Suckers from the stock should be looked after; and whether from above or under ground, be invariably destroyed. It will also be found beneficial to keep the surface of the soil constantly in a loose state.

TYING UP AND TRAINING.

As the plants advance in growth, some will require sticks to keep the shoots apart and support the flowers. The few which hold their flowers gracefully, and shew themselves well, are not, perhaps, improved by being drawn from their natural position of growth; but where the flowers do not shew themselves to advantage, or the shoots become much crowded, the plants may be improved in appearance, and really benefited, by drawing the lower shoots downwards towards the edge of the pot, where they may be fastened to a piece of bast or wire, made to pass beneath the rim: the upper shoots may then be drawn out to sticks. A neat hoop, fixed horizontally about the centre of the head of the plant, admits of a very pretty method of arrangement. If the plant be large, two, or even three hoops may be requisite, to which the shoots should be drawn, inclined downwards, as they are, when growing, sure to rise sufficiently. This—the circular method of training—is the most natural one; but for the sake of effect, when intended for exhibition, the plants are sometimes trained to a face, so that all the flowers may be seen from one point at the same time. This is, to use a familiar expression, certainly placing the best side towards London, and would doubtless be an excellent method, if we could always hide the back of the plant, and feel satisfied with growing half plants instead of whole ones. Our favourite form for most varieties is a pyramid; and as the fashioning of the plant is partly accomplished by pruning, we revert for a moment to that operation.

The accompanying illustration (No. 1) is intended to shew a plant two years old that has just completed its growth. The intersecting lines shew the manner in which it should be pruned. Thinning has been superseded by disbudding during the season of growth. Immediately after pruning, the shoots should be drawn as near to a horizontal position as possible without straining them, and left so until the eyes have pushed to the length of half an inch: the plant may then be brought back to its natural form.

The next cut (No. 2) shews the state of this plant in the season of bloom. But it is not yet perfect. It requires another year's growth.

No. 1. Pyramid of two years' growth.

In the next cut (No. 3) we see it pruned, trained, and commencing the third year's growth. The form is easy and graceful, and by it the shoots, leaves, and flowers are shewn to advantage, and are open to the beneficial influences of the sun and air.

But there are some kinds of very dwarf growth, for which the pyramidal form of training is not the most advantageous. Such should be trained as round bushes.

The accompanying illustrations (Nos. 4 and 5) will convey our idea of the form they should assume better than a detailed account of treatment. This indeed would be nearly a repetition of the last mode. The difference is, they require shortening to two, three, or four eyes, in order to preserve

No. 2.   Pyramid of two years' growth in bloom.

the plant handsome, and develope the eyes capable of producing the finest flowers. As the shoots rarely exceed a few inches in growth, and the eyes are remarkably close together, the plant must, if treated thus, always remain of lowly growth. Our last sketch (No. 4) represented a full-

No. 3. Pyramid of three year's growth, pruned.

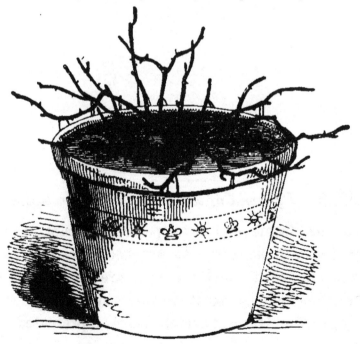

No. 4. Bush-rose pruned.

grown Bush-rose newly pruned; the present sketch (No. 5) represents the same in flower.

No. 5.   Bush-rose in bloom.

SHADING.

When the plants commence flowering, it will be necessary to shade them during the middle of the day; or if a house with a north aspect is vacant, where they can be fully exposed to light, yet shaded from the sun, they should be removed thither a few days before coming into flower. By this plan the plant remains longer in bloom, the flowers grow to a larger size, and retain their brilliancy for a longer period.

REPOTTING.

This operation may be performed at any season of the year. When the pot becomes crowded with roots, the plant should be shifted. It is our practice to glance over the stock occasionally in the summer months; and whenever a plant is observed growing vigorously, it is at once removed to a larger pot. But it is of the general re-potting that we would now more especially speak. Every plant should be repotted at least once a year, and the most advantageous time is, perhaps, September. A good portion of the old soil should be shaken away in the operation: all wild suckers should be eradicated, worms withdrawn, and such plants as require it replaced in larger pots.

CHOICE OF VARIETIES.

We will now proceed to describe a few kinds which appear best calculated for growing in pots.

To select varieties to meet the concurrence of all cultivators, is, I fear, a difficult task, if not impracticable; so much in flowers depending on taste, that probably no two persons, though equally well acquainted with Roses, would select the same kinds.

CHARACTERISTICS OF VARIETIES SUITED FOR POT-CULTURE.

In searching out the following, from an immense number of varieties which I have had constant opportunities of looking over while in bloom, I have endeavoured to hold in view the following points:—

1. Elegance of habit, regarding both growth and flowering.
2. Contrast of colour.
3. Abundance of bloom.
4. Form or outline of the individual flower.
5. Duration of bloom.
6. Sweetness.

Probably few given will have a claim on all these points: some combine them more intimately than others.

The *habit* of a plant is always deserving of regard, and especially when intended to be grown in a pot. A Rose cannot be good for this purpose, however beautiful the flower, unless the *tout ensemble* is elegant. As a class of Roses, the Bourbon Perpetuals may perhaps be given as a standard of habit, but they cannot vie with the Hybrid Perpetuals in richness and splendour. The latter, the Hybrid Bourbon, and the Tea-scented, stand highest in rank as Pot-Roses.

In a collection, *contrast of colour* is of undoubted import; and some will probably be found selected on account of their distinctness, which otherwise would not have found place here.

With regard to flowering, *many of our profuse blooming Roses are not the most double*, nor the finest in form; but the magnificent appearance they present as pot plants, when viewed *en masse*, may perhaps be considered a sufficient plea for their insertion. These, however, which are few in number, may be distinguished throughout the list by the prefix of an asterisk.

There are various styles of Roses, each good in its way. Whether the *form* be cupped, globular, or compact, the outline should be circular, and the petals smooth and round at their circumference.

By *duration of bloom*, allusion is more particularly made to the length of time the flowers continue in perfection when open, than to succession of flower. Juno (Hybrid Bourbon), for example, and, in fact, most thick-petalled Roses, hold their flowers in perfection for some days; whereas others fall almost as soon as expanded. Now, to

c

obtain a number of flowers on one plant, in all the various stages of bloom, at a given time, is one great point the cultivator of Roses in pots, for exhibition, has to attend to. Therefore, both among Summer and Autumn Roses, such as are for some time in perfection as buds, and when expanded remain for some time in perfection as flowers, are considered the most desirable.

Scent, which is an inestimable property of a Rose, needs no comment.

CLASSES PREFERRED.

The classes of Roses that can be practically recommended for growing in pots, are, Moss, Provence, Hybrid Perpetual, Hybrids of the Chinese and Bourbon, Noisette, Bourbon, Chinese, and Tea-scented. The Boursault, Ayrshire, and Sempervirens, are pretty, grown as climbers, but are not fitted for exhibition.

Moss. *Blooming in summer only.*—The Moss Rose, which is supposed to be an accidental variation of the Provence, is a very general favourite: it delights in a rich soil, and thrives best on its own roots, or budded on very short stems. There are but few varieties that can be recommended for Pot-culture: still, these few, cast among the many, give a great degree of distinctness to a collection; and they certainly cannot be dispensed with anywhere:—

Common; pale rose, beautiful, large and full.*
Crested; rose, beautiful, large and full.

---

* The prices of the varieties throughout may be obtained by consulting the Rose Catalogue published annually in September, and transmissible gratis, per post, on application at the Nurseries, Waltham Cross, London, N.

Gloire des Mousseuses; blush, very large and full, one of the best.

Gracilis, or Prolific; deep pink, free bloomer, large and full.

Laneii; rosy crimson, tinted with purple, large and full.

PROVENCE. *Blooming in summer only.*—This is an excellent class of Roses for growing in pots; and the old Cabbage Rose must not be excluded. The whole of them are sweet—very sweet; and their pendulous growth gives to them a very graceful appearance. The flowers are large, well-formed, and, in shape, mostly globular.

Cabbage, or Common; rosy pink, large and full.
White Provence; pure white, large and full.

HYBRID PERPETUAL. *Blooming in summer and autumn.*— These Roses have become universal favourites, and deservedly so. Their foliage is beautiful, and the flowers of some kinds are finely shaped. The rapid influx of new varieties has increased and improved this class surprisingly within the last few years. They have hitherto been too much of one colour—crimson purple; but this is now partly remedied, and there doubtless will soon be as great a variety here as in other classes. Some of these will be given as Pyramid Roses, for which they are well suited, blooming fine both in summer and autumn. They are excellent Forcing Roses, hardy, and very sweet.

Alphonse Damaizin; brilliant shaded crimson, good form and habit.

* Anna Alexieff; pretty rose colour, large, full, and of good habit, flowers freely.

Anna de Diesbach; clear rose, fine colour very large and showy.

Auguste Mie; light pink, large, full and good.

Baron Adolphe de Rothschild; fiery red, petals often edged with white: large, full, and very effective.

Baron Pelletan de Kinkelin; crimson and purple shaded, colours brilliant, large, full, and of fine form.

Baronne Prévost; pale rose, superb, very large and full.

Beauty of Waltham (Wm. Paul); cherry colour to carmine, large and full, form cupped, very hardy: one of the loveliest and sweetest, blooming abundantly.

Black Prince (Wm. Paul); scarlet crimson, shaded with black, globular, large and full, unique in colour, perfect in form.

Cardinal Patrizzi; brilliant red, shaded, full, fine.

Caroline de Sansal; clear flesh-colour, edges blush, very large and full.

Charles Margottin; brilliant carmine, centre fiery red, very large, full, and sweet, outer petals large and round: of the race of "Jules Margottin:" one of the best.

Claude Million; scarlet crimson dashed with rose and violet, velvety, large, full, and of excellent form, habit good.

Comtesse de Chabrillant; pink, beautifully cupped, large and full, very sweet and good.

Denis Helye; brilliant rosy carmine, lovely colour, very large and full, very effective.

Dr. Lindley (Wm. Paul); flowers crimson, with black centres, very large and full, growth robust, foliage splendid.

Elizabeth Vigneron (Wm. Paul); flowers rosy pink, very large and full, cupped in the way of "Lælia," but fuller, fresher, and brighter in colour: constitution hardy, blooms continually: one of the best.

François Lacharme; bright carmine, changing to red, full and globular: a superb rose.

* Géant des Batailles, brilliant crimson shaded with purple, large and very double.

General d' Hautpoult; brilliant reddish scarlet, the centre-petals sometimes striped with white, large, full, and of globular form, one of the best.

* General Jacqueminot; brilliant red, velvety, large and double.

Glory of Waltham (Wm. Paul); crimson, large, full, and of fine form and habit.

Jean Goujon; beautiful clear red, very large, full and good.

Jean Rosenkrantz; beautiful coral red, large, full, and of perfect form: one of the best.

Jean Touvais; beautiful reddish purple, shaded with crimson, very large, full, and of excellent form: blooms freely.

John Hopper; rose, crimson centre, reverse of the petals purplish lilac: large and full.

* Jules Margottin; bright cherry, large and full: a superb rose.

Kate Hausburg; fine bright rose, large, full, and of excellent shape and substance.

La Brillante; transparent carmine, very bright and beautiful, large and of fine form.

Lælia; shaded rose, very large, full, and of fine form.

Le Rhone; vermillion, colour rich and brilliant, large, full, and of good form: one of the best.

Lord Raglan; scarlet crimson, edges violet crimson, large and full.

Lord Macaulay (Wm. Paul); rich scarlet crimson, sometimes maroon crimson, large and full, petals of great substance, good habit, foliage handsome: a first-class rose.

Madame Alfred de Rougemont; pure white, lightly and delicately shaded with rose and carmine, large and full, shape of the "Cabbage Rose:" one of the best.

Madame Boll; rose colour, sometimes edged with blush, a large, full, and handsome rose.

Madame Charles Verdier; fine vermeil rose, very large, full, and of fine form, very sweet, damask scented: one of the best.

Madame Charles Wood; vinous crimson, very large, full, and effective.

Madame Clemence Joigneaux; red shaded with lilac: large, full, and fine.

Madame Derreux Douville; delicate glossy rose, bordered with white, large, full, of fine form, and good habit.

Madame Domage; bright rose, very large and double.

Madame Emile Boyau, (Wm. Paul); flowers soft rosy flesh colour, changing to blush, sufficiently large, perfect in form, constitution hardy, growth moderate: very constant, distinct, and good.

Madame Rousset; beautiful pink, the reverse of the petals silvery, large, full, finely cupped, and good habit: one of the best.

Madame Victor Verdier; rich bright rosy cherry colour, large, full, and of fine form, cupped, blooms in clusters.

Maréchal Souchet; beautiful reddish crimson, shaded with dark maroon, very large and full, petals also large, habit good: one of the best.

Mrs. William Paul; bright violet red, shaded with fiery

red, flowers constantly and in clusters, large and full: one of the best.

Paul Delameilleray; fine purplish cerise, very large, full, and of excellent form.

Pierre Notting; blackish red shaded with violet, very large and full, form globular, habit good : one of the best.

Prince Camille de Rohan; crimson maroon shaded with blood red, very rich and velvety, large and full, distinct and good.

Princess of Wales, (W^m. Paul); vivid crimson, presenting to the eye an unusual body of colour owing to the thickness of the petals, cupped, large, very double, and remarkably smooth, free, hardy, and of good habit.

Semiramis; clear pink, blush edges, large, full, and of fine globular form : one of the best.

Senatéur Vaisse; bright red, large, and very double : superb.

Victor Verdier; rosy carmine, purplish edges, a large, showy, free growing rose, of good quality and very effective.

BOURBON PERPETUAL. *Blooming in summer and autumn.*—These Roses, although of smaller size than those of the preceding group, are by no means of less merit, being mostly of fine form and habit, and producing a profusion of distinct and beautiful flowers.

Baronne Noirmont; deep rose, large, and of good form.
Catherine Guillot; deep pink, perfect form : one of the best.

Comtesse Barbantanne; flesh-colour, large, full, and of fine form, free and good.

Emotion; white tinted with rose, of medium size, full, form perfect, flowers abundantly.

L'Avenir; glossy pink, large, full, and of fine form.

Louise Margottin; delicate satin-like rose, of medium size and exquisite form.

Louise Odier; fine bright rose, full, very free bloomer.

Madame de Stella; bright rose, large, full, and of fine form.

Mademoiselle Emain; white, rosy centre, full, and of good form.

Michel Bonnet; beautiful rosy peach, large and full: one of the best.

Modéle de Perfection; lively pink, very pretty, blooms freely: one of the best.

* Rev. H. Dombrain; carmine, large and cupped, blooms freely.

HYBRIDS OF THE CHINESE AND BOURBON. *Blooming in summer only.*—Many of this class are profuse bloomers, the flowers are large, and some, perfect models of form. The Hybrid Bourbons are remarkable for their robust habit and bold foliage; they are perfectly hardy, and require but little pruning. Many of them form fine Pyramid Roses in pots.

Charles Lawson; vivid rose, shaded, large and full: one of the best.

Coupe d'Hébé; rich deep pink, large and very double: one of the best.

Juno; pale rose, blush edges, very large and full.

* Paul Perras, beautiful pale rose, fine, very large and full.

Paul Ricaut; bright rosy crimson, large and full: one of the best.

William Jesse; purplish crimson tinged with lilac, superb, very large and very double.

NOISETTE. *Blooming in summer and autumn.*—On account of blooming fine so late in the season, the Noisettes form a very valuable class of Roses. The most of them are better trained spirally, in which way their large trusses of bloom produce a very pleasing effect. Under that method of growth, then, we shall class the most of them, but a few may be retained here.

* Aimée Vibert; pure white, beautiful, full.
* Caroline Marniesse; blush white, blooming in clusters.

Celine Forestier; pale yellow, free bloomer, large and full.

Lamarque; sulphur yellow, beautiful, very large and full.

Solfaterre; fine sulphur yellow, large and very double.

Triomphe de Rennes; canary, large, full, and fine.

BOURBON. *Blooming in summer and autumn.*—This class of Roses is truly elegant. The varieties, originally of one colour only, are now well varied, by the introduction of many purple, crimson, and blush roses. Before the appearance of these, the Bourbons were nearly all of a rose colour. Probably the dark varieties now obtained have something of the Chinese in them; but this crossing slightly affects their hardiness, though in most points they rival, and, in one point (profusion of bloom), surpass their Bourbon parent. The colours of the Bourbon Roses are very clear; the petals are smooth, thick, large, and generally well-formed; the foliage broad and handsome. The small growers require close pruning. They are beautiful Pot-Roses, but do not generally attain to sufficient size to be grown as exhibition plants. To this remark, however, "Souvenir de Malmaison" is a splendid exception.

Docteur Lepreste; bright purplish red, shaded.
* Dupetit Thouars; beautiful bright crimson, large and full.
George Peabody; purplish crimson, cupped, large and full.
Leon Oursel; light red, large, full, and good.
Marquis Balbiano; rose tinged with silver, full, fine form, distinct.
* Queen; buff rose, free bloomer, large and double.
Souvenir de Malmaison; clear flesh-colour, edges blush, beautiful, very large and full.
* Victor Emmanuel; purple and purplish maroon, large and double, good and distinct.

(*T.*) Chinese or Bengalese. *Blooming in summer and autumn.*—Although less hardy than the last group, these are very valuable among the Autumnal Roses, being continually in flower. They group admirably with the Tea-scented; and their colours being, in part, those which are deficient among the latter, they are the more desirable. They delight in a rich soil, require close pruning, and, when grown in pots, succeed best on their own roots.

There is a pretty variation belonging to the Chinese, known as the Lawrenciana, or Fairy Rose. These are not suited for exhibition, as they are of very small growth, rarely exceeding a few inches in height when grown in pots. A few varieties will be given here; for when the plants become of some size, and are covered with their diminutive buds and blossoms, they are really interesting objects. They delight in a light sandy soil.

   Archduke Charles; pale shaded rose, changing to crimson.
   Cramoisie supèrieure; rich velvety crimson, beautiful, full.
   Eugène Beauharnais; amaranth, superb, large and full.
   Madame Bréon; beautiful rich rose, large and full.
   Marjolin du Luxembourg; dark crimson, superb, very large and full.
   * Mrs. Bosanquet; delicate pale flesh, large and double.

LAWRENCIANAS.

   Alba Minor; white.
   Fairy; pale rose.
   Pumila; rose.
   Rubra; brilliant crimson.

(*T.*) TEA-SCENTED. *Blooming in summer and autumn.*— These are, in fact, but a selection from the Chinese, on account of their delicious odour and shining foliage. The flowers are mostly large: the tints of some are remarkably rich, of others as peculiarly soft and delicate. Every collection of Pot-Roses should include a quantity of these, as they become of greatly increased beauty under this system of culture, and moreover cannot be depended on when grown in the open ground. They vary much *in degree* of hardiness and sweetness, but all are tender and all are sweet. Many are excellent for forcing.

   Alba Rosea; white, centre rose, large, full, and very sweet.
   Bougère; deep rosy bronze, superb, very large and full.

Comte de Paris; flesh-coloured rose, superb, very large and full.

Comtesse de Brossard; bright yellow, large and full.

Devoniensis; pale yellow, superb, very large and full.

Enfant de Lyon; pale yellow, large and full.

Gloire de Dijon; yellow, shaded with salmon, very large and full: a superb rose.

Julie Mansais; pure white, large and full.

Louise de Savoie; fine yellow, large and full.

Madame Bravy; creamy white, large and full, perfect shape.

* Madame Damaizin; salmon, large and full, free bloomer, and hardy.

Madame Falcot; yellow, in the way of "Safrano," but of a deeper shade, and more double.

Madame de St. Joseph; salmon pink, beautiful, very large and double, very sweet.

Madame Halphin; salmon pink, centre yellowish, large and full.

Madame Villermoz; white, centre salmon, large, full, and good.

Maréchal Niel; beautiful deep yellow, large, full, and of globular form, very sweet, the shoots well clothed with large shining leaves.

* Marquise de Foucault; white, fawn, and yellow, variable, large and double.

Narcisse; fine pale yellow, large and full.

Niphetos; pale lemon, often snowy white, very large and full.

President; rose shaded with salmon, very large, and of good form.

Rubens; white, shaded with rose, yellowish centre, large, full, and of fine form.

* Safrano; bright apricot in bud, changing to buff.

Souvenir d'Elise Vardon; creamy white, centre yellowish, very large and full: a splendid rose.

Souvenir d'Un Ami; salmon and rose shaded, large and full, fine.

Vicomtesse de Cazes; yellow, centre deeper yellow, tinted with copper colour, large and very double.

The letter *T*, preceding any class, indicates that the varieties of which it is composed require protection from frost in winter.

YELLOW ROSES.

Since the first edition of this little work was penned, Yellow Roses have become a special branch of culture. Separate prizes have been offered for them by the London Horticultural and Royal Botanic Societies. But what are Yellow Roses? This question provoked some discussion in the pages of the "Gardeners' Journal" in 1849, through the withholding of a prize by the Royal Botanic Society. To prevent any misconception at future exhibitions, that Society named the varieties considered eligible for competition. Some of these have since become obsolete, but we reproduce here varieties within the same range of colour.

Yellow Banksiæ.
Williams's Double Yellow (Austrian).
Harrisonii (ditto).
Persian Yellow (ditto).
Cloth of Gold (Noisette).
Solfaterre (ditto).
Celine Forestier (ditto).

Isabella Gray (Noisette).
Jane Hardy (ditto).
Triomphe de Rennes (ditto).
Narcisse (Tea-scented).
Vicomtesse de Cazes (ditto).
Jaune, or Yellow China (ditto).
Comtesse de Brossard (ditto).
Gloire de Dijon (ditto).
Jaune d'Or (ditto).
La Boule d'Or (ditto).
Lays (ditto).
Madame Falcot (ditto).
Madame Lartay (ditto).
Mdlle. Adele Jougant (ditto).
Marcèhal Niel (ditto).

We now proceed to analyze this group. The first on the list—the Yellow Banksiæ—is a pretty enough Rose, with small flowers produced in clusters. It may be grown well in a soil composed of equal parts of loam, peat, and leaf-mould. It requires but little pruning: the mere tips of the shoots may be taken off. Spiral training is recommended as the most suitable. The succeeding three varieties are nearly allied in nature, and may be grown in a soil similar to the last, but the addition of sand, unless the peat or loam be sandy, will prove advantageous. Very little pruning is necessary: some of the shoots may be cut out entirely; the others have their mere ends taken off. If grown on their own roots they may be trained as globular or columnar bushes: if grown on stems the branches may be drawn downwards in the form of a Weeping Rose. The two next in order—Cloth of Gold and Solfaterre—are of vigorous growth, producing large flowers of great beauty. Both are shy bloomers, especially the former. The same soil as recommended in the early part of this treatise for Pot-Roses in general may be used for these and the other varieties of "Noisette." Little pruning is necessary, and spiral training is recommended. The remaining 12 varieties belong to the Tea-scented, which require a rich soil and close pruning. The most advantageous systems of training these are the round bush or the pyramid. Were this group to be viewed critically, it might be said they are not all "purely yellow." It might also be said there are kinds excluded which have as just a right to the appellation of "yellow" as they. But when it is considered that the declension from yellow to white and buff is so gradual that it is scarcely possible to fix the line of demarcation, and that a list of twenty-two varieties is given from which to select six, these points of criticism are hardly tenable. If none others are allowed to be exhibited, or none whose flowers are less yellow when brought to the exhibition tables than those above enumerated, the practical utility of the arrangement will soon become apparent.*

CLIMBERS.

Climbing Roses should be invariably grown on their own roots; and being chiefly kept in pots, their cultivation may commence at any season we please. What we have hitherto been accustomed to regard as Climbers are from the classes Boursault, Sempervirens, Ayrshire, &c. Magnificent as such must be regarded when growing in the

---

* We retain these remarks on "Yellow Roses" although they are now seldom made the subject of special prizes at the London Flower Shows.—W. P.

open ground, often to the height of twenty feet, and covered with immense trusses of bloom, their semi-double and transient flowers render the greater part not altogether suitable for growing in pots. A growth not too vigorous, and finely-shaped flowers, should be the criteria with regard to Roses grown in pots as Climbers. As a great height is not in this instance desirable, the various Hybrids, the Noisettes, and Bourbons, may be chosen, and trained upwards to about four feet, which will probably be found as high as convenient or manageable: not that we would, however, altogether exclude the Ayrshire and Sempervirens, for among them a few admirable Roses are to be found.

Now one great point to be held in view in regard to this system of culture is, to induce the plants to flower from the summit to the ground; for if a few flowers only are to be produced at the top of the plant, then the dwarfer it can be grown the better. This complete flowering judicious pruning and training will accomplish.

TRAINING AND PRUNING CLIMBERS.

In training, they may be formed into any shape. Such varieties as have long twining or flexible shoots may be trained spirally; with which view, in pruning, in the first instance, they should be cut-in close, to induce them to form lengthened shoots, which should be trained in their proper course during the season of growth.

The annexed engraving represents a plant two years old. It is autumn, and it has completed the second year's growth. But we look back to the end of the first year's growth in order to speak of the manner in which it was treated in pruning. It then had several weak shoots,

These were all cut away but two; one of which was cut back to a single eye which produced the lower shoot of the present engraving (No. 6); the other, being a short shoot,

No. 6. *Twiner pruned.*

with a terminal bud, was not shortened at all; and this, as may be observed, produced two shoots. By this treatment no flowers were produced; but a strong well-ordered plant was obtained in a short space of time. Now let us look to the future. The main object in pruning now is to obtain flowers. To secure this end, the three leading shoots may be shortened level with the tops of the sticks; the lateral shoot (there is but one in this instance) cut back to four or five eyes; and the probable result will be, a tree covered with bloom, resembling, in some measure, the accompanying engraving. (No. 7.)

No. 7. *Twiner in bloom.*

Under this mode of growth a small amount of pruning is necessary: any superfluous or crowded shoots may of course be removed; and however many laterals there may be, the whole should be cut back to three, four, or five eyes, according to their strength of growth.

The stiff, erect growing kinds may be formed into short pillars, or trained to flat wires. The former present the most natural appearance; and, to effect this, from three to five shoots may be allowed in the first instance, and pruned of different lengths: these will throw out laterals, and if tied round a single stick placed in the centre of the pot, a column or pillar of roses is formed. In after seasons they may be pruned, as proposed for other Roses.

CLIMBING VARIETIES.

Here, then, is a list of such varieties as appear best adapted for this purpose.

HYBRIDS OF THE CHINESE AND BOURBON.

Blairii, No. 2; blush pink, fine, very large and double.

Brennus or Brutus; deep carmine, superb, very large and full.

Charles Lawson; vivid rose, shaded, large and full: one of the best.

Chénédolé; light vivid crimson, colour exquisite, very large and double: a fine Pillar Rose.

Coupe d' Hébé; rich deep pink, large and very double: one of the best.

General Jacqueminot; purplish crimson, large and full, fine.

Madame Plantier; pure white, free bloomer, beautiful and full.

Paul Perras; pale rose, fine, very large and full.

Vivid, (Paul); rich vivid crimson, very showy: a good Pillar or Climbing Rose.

AYRSHIRE.

Bennett's Seedling; white, small and double.

Dundee Rambler; white, semi-double.

Splendens; white, edged with red, semi-double.

SEMPERVIRENS.

Félicité Perpetué; creamy white, beautiful, small and full.

Flora; bright rose, full, and of fine colour.

Leopoldine d'Orleans; white, shaded with rose, beautiful, double.

HYBRID PERPETUAL.

Admiral Nelson; crimson, colour beautiful.

Centifolia Rosea; bright pink, large, of beautiful cupped form.

Duc de Cazes; blackish velvety purple, globular, large and full.

Duc de Rohan; red, shaded with vermilion, bright, large and full, form good, foliage handsome.

Glory of Waltham, (Wm. Paul); flowers crimson, in the way of "Red Rover," but more double, growth of extraordinary vigour: one of the best of Pillar or Climbing Roses.

Le Baron de Rothschild; dark reddish carmine, sometimes shaded with violet, very large and full.

Madame Hector Jacquin; clear rose, shaded with lilac, large and full.

Madame Julie Daran; purplish vermilion, glossy, very large and full: one of the best.

Maréchal Vaillant; purplish red, very large, full, and of good form.

Maurice Bernardin; vermilion, large, full, and of fine form: one of the best.

Red Rover, (Wm. Paul); fiery red, growth more than usually vigorous, flowering up to Christmas.

Souvenir de la Reine d'Angleterre; bright rose, large and full, very effective.

BOURBON PERPETUAL.

Catherine Guillot; deep pink, perfect form: one of the best.

Comtesse Barbantanne; flesh-colour, large, full, and of fine form, free and good.

L'Avenir; glossy pink, large, full, and of fine form.

ROSE DE ROSOMENE.

Gloire de Rosomene; brilliant carmine, large and semi-double: a good autumn-blooming Climbing Rose.

Oriflamme de St. Louis; brilliant carmine, large and double.

BOURBON.

Bouquet de Flore; bright rosy carmine.

Empress Eugenie; pale rose, purple edges, large and full.

Pierre de St. Cyr; pink, large and full.

Sir Joseph Paxton; bright rose, shaded with crimson, large and full.

NOISETTE.

Aimee Vibert; pure white, beautiful, full.

Caroline Marniesse; blush white, blooming in clusters.

Celine Forestier; pale yellow, free bloomer, large and full.

Cloth of Gold; yellow, edges sulphur, large and double.

Desprez à fleur jaune; red, buff, and sulphur, variable, very sweet, large and full.

Du Luxembourg; lilac rose, centre deep red, large.

Fellenberg; rosy crimson, very free bloomer.

Isabella Gray; yellow, large and full.

Jane Hardy; golden yellow, large and full.

Lamarque; sulphur yellow, beautiful, very large and full.

Madame Massot; pure white, centre flesh-colour, small, finely formed, blooms in large clusters and very freely.

Mdlle. Aristide; pale yellow, centre salmon, large and full.

Ophirie; nankeen and copper, distinct, full.

Solfaterre; fine sulphur yellow, large, and very double.

TEA SCENTED.

Climbing Devoniensis; identical with the old "Devoniensis" in flower, but of a rapid running growth, and hence valuable as a climber.

Gloire de Dijon; yellow, shaded with salmon, very large and full: a superb Rose.

Homer; rose, centre salmon, variable, large, full and good.

Maréchal Niel; beautiful deep yellow, large, full, and of globular form, very sweet, the shoots well clothed with large shining leaves.

Triomphe de Guillot fils; white, shaded with rose and salmon, very large, full, and sweet: one of the best.

FORCING.

Roses required for forcing will succeed tolerably well if potted early in the preceding autumn. It is, however, obvious, that, by being potted a twelvemonth previously, they become thoroughly established, and are better enabled to support an accelerated growth and premature development of bloom. *If, therefore, we are anxious to obtain a perfect bloom of forced Roses, and have plants that have been a twelvemonth or more in pots, they should certainly be taken in preference, and the fresh-potted ones be allowed to grow on for the natural season of flowering.* Presuming, then, the plants about to be forced have been grown one year in pots, we will proceed with our subject.

FORCING-HOUSE.

A span-roofed house, with a longer roof towards the south, is perhaps the best style of building. The interior may be fitted up according to the taste of the proprietor.

The various systems of heating horticultural buildings now in vogue have been frequently descanted on in the gardening periodicals, and it would be out of place to speak of them here, except in general terms. Heating by hot water, in its various modes of application, is generally acknowledged to be preferable to the old flue system, and in no instance is it more so than for forcing Roses: nevertheless, they will flower well in houses heated with flues. When the latter mode is adopted, syringing should be more freely resorted to; and a pot or two of water, poured down on the floor of the house every morning, is necessary to keep a moist atmosphere, which is very favourable to forced Roses, and, at the same time, noxious to the red spider, which is very likely to appear under the flue system of heating. Arnott's stove, which is used by some, is found to answer exceedingly well.

RIPENING THE WOOD.

It is important, with regard to Roses intended for

forcing, that the wood be well ripened *early in autumn;* and, to effect this end, they should be placed in a sunny and airy situation during summer, and should not have too free a supply of water when *completing* their growth. So soon as they have done growing, they may be thinned out, as previously proposed; the shortening-in of the shoots being deferred till the plants are conveyed into the forcing-house.

HOUSING THE PLANTS.

The last week in December is an excellent time for this purpose, commencing with a gentle heat. It is advisable to keep the plants as close to the glass as possible; and if a gentle bottom heat can be secured, so much the better. At first the fire should be lighted of a morning, and kept in for a few hours only, to throw a little warmth into the house, and no air need be admitted. When the buds begin to swell, the heat may be steadily increased till we reach 60° to 65° by day, and the night temperature should never be lower than 45°; a difference of 15° or 20° between the day and night temperature proving beneficial. If, on entering the forcing-house, there is discovered a freshness and glaucous hue on the leaves, we may rest satisfied that the atmosphere and temperature are agreeable to the plants. But should the leaves droop and present a flabby appearance, we should attribute this to too dry an atmosphere, or too high a temperature maintained at night. The remedy is easy.

ADMISSION OF AIR.

Early in the season it is well to be cautious in the admission of air; for the young leaves of forced Roses are very tender, and suffer much from the cold. As the season advances top air may be given for a few hours in the middle of the day, in still mild weather, with great benefit to the plants; but in cold weather air should be admitted from the lower part of the house only; and if it can be made to pass over the pipes or flue on entering, that it may become more thoroughly amalgamated with the warm air of the house before reaching the leaves, so much the better.

SYRINGING.

In bright weather the plants should be freely syringed morning and evening: in dull weather very lightly, and once only; soot-water may be used here with good effect.

INSECTS—MILDEW.

The green fly is a great pest among forced Roses, but is easily destroyed by fumigating with tobacco, which should be done as soon as any of them are seen, and repeated as often as they re-appear.

The plan of fumigating usually practised is one so unpleasant, that we believe the greatest lover of "the noxious weed" would rather be a spectator than an operator. It is, therefore, with much pleasure that we are enabled, through the kindness of a friend, to communicate a method practised by him, by which the destruction of the aphis is accomplished, while the operator escapes unscathed. Some sheets of brown paper, the thicker in moderation the better, are soaked in a saturated solution of nitre. These are, after a short period, laid by to dry, and, *if found to burn freely without flame*, pronounced ready for use. On each piece is laid a thin layer of tobacco, and the paper is rolled round on a stick in the way in which music is usually rolled up, taking care to maintain an equal distribution of the tobacco in the operation. The roll is then tied in two or three places to keep it fixed, and the stick being withdrawn, the former is suspended by a wire from any part of the house, so that the lower end nearly reaches the ground. The lower end is lighted, and, as the combustion proceeds, the fumes gradually disperse, and the ashes drop on the ground. One, two, or three of these may be used, according to their size, or the size of the house to be fumigated.

Another annoyance is the grub, with which most Rose cultivators are too familiar, and whose ravages, if not stopped, will, as well as destroying the leaves and causing the plants to look shabby, materially injure the bloom. Wherever the leaves are curled, or found sticking together, this insect will be comfortably rolled up within, and not unfrequently does it ensconce itself in the growing point of a young shoot. The plants must be looked over frequently, to reduce these destructive visitants, and they require to be very closely sought.

Every precaution should be taken against mildew. If the weather be cloudy and wet, a brisk heat should be maintained, that we may not have a *cold*, damp atmosphere. The house ought also to be swept out frequently, and kept clean. Probably the close atmosphere in which the plants are necessarily grown during the early part of the forcing season contributes, in no small degree, to encourage mildew: if it does appear, it is seldom till late in the season, when the plants have been in the house some length of time. The application of sulphur is a well-known remedy, dusted on the leaves, while wet, from a dredging-box; and by admitting abundance of air, and at the same time applying fire-heat should the house be damp, to establish a free circulation among the plants, its progress will certainly be arrested.

SUCKERS.

Among the worked plants, an eye should be had to suckers, which may, when young, be radically removed by clasping them firmly between the thumb and finger, and drawing them steadily out.

WATERING.

During their growth, the plants should be freely watered; occasionally with guano-water, about the temperature of the house; or, if worms work in the pots, lime-water is an efficient remedy.

SEASON OF FLOWERING.

Late in February a few precocious flower-buds will expand. By the middle of March the plants will probably be in full bloom, when syringing may be dispensed with for a time. A slight shading will be found necessary during the middle of the day, to prevent the flowers flagging, and fire-heat should be in some degree diminished.

A continual succession of flowers may be obtained, by removing some of the plants, at different periods, as the buds shew colour, to a house of a lower temperature. This will also be the means of increasing the size and deepening the tints of the flowers.

Now, as soon as the plants have flowered, such as are termed Summer Roses (those blooming but once in the season) may be removed to a cold pit or house, to make room for the admission of fresh plants kept in reserve for the purpose.

PRUNING AUTUMNALS FOR SECOND BLOOM.

When the March-flowering is over, the shoots of the Autumnal, or perpetual-flowering kinds, may be cut back, and they will give forth a second crop of flowers in fine perfection by the end of May. Many, if not pruned, would continue flowering: but pruning is recommended, if care be taken to remove no more leaves than is necessary in the operation. After April, very little fire-heat is required, especially if the weather be warm and sunny; and after flowering a second time, the plants may be removed from the house, the top of the soil loosened, a little manure spread on the surface, and the pots plunged in an airy situation, there to remain till required for forcing the succeeding year. Thus treated, the plants may be induced to flower well, forced several years in succession.

FORCING VARIETIES.

The following varieties are of the best description for forcing, and in their selection I have been guided by the same principles before advanced, leaning, perhaps, more particularly to sweetness; at the same time maintaining, that it is better to have one first-rate Rose growing in two positions, than a greater variety comprising kinds of inferior merit.

PROVENCE.

Cabbage or common; rosy pink, large and full.

MOSS.

Common; pale rose, beautiful, large and full.

Crested; rose, beautiful, large, and full.

Gracilis, or Prolific; deep pink, free bloomer, large, and full.

HYBRID CHINESE AND BOURBON.

Charles Lawson; vivid rose, shaded, large and full: one of the best.

Coupe d' Hébé; rich deep pink, large and very double: one of the best.

Juno; pale rose, blush edges, very large and full.

Paul Perras; pale rose, fine, very large and full.

Paul Ricaut; bright rosy crimson, large and full: one of the best.

William Jesse; purplish crimson, tinged with lilac, superb, very large and very double.

HYBRID PERPETUAL.

Anna Alexieff; rose colour, large, full, and of good habit: flowers freely.

Anna de Diesbach; clear rose, fine colour, very large and showy.

Auguste Mie; light pink, large, full, and good.

Baronne Prevost; pale rose, superb, very large and full.

Beauty of Waltham (Wm. Paul); cherry colour to bright carmine, large and full, form, cupped, very hardy: one of the loveliest and sweetest, blooming abundantly.

Bernard Palissy; bright carmine, large, full, and very fine: good habit.

Charles Margottin; brilliant carmine, centre fiery red, very large, full, and sweet, outer petals large and round: of the race of "Jules Margottin:" one of the best.

Comtesse de Chabrillant; pink, beautifully cupped, large and full, very sweet and good.

Elizabeth Vigneron (Wm. Paul); flowers rosy pink, very large and full, cupped in the way of "Lælia," but fuller, fresher, and brighter in colour, constitution hardy, growth vigorous, blooms continuously: one of the best.

François Lacharme; bright carmine, changing to red, full and globular: a superb rose.

Géant des Batailles; brilliant crimson, shaded with purple, large and very double.

General Jacqueminot; brilliant red, velvety, large and double.

Jean Touvais; beautiful reddish purple, shaded with crimson, very large, full, and of excellent form, blooms freely.

John Hopper; rose, crimson centre, reverse of the petals purplish lilac, large and full.

Jules Margottin; bright cherry, large and full: a superb rose.

Kate Hausburg; fine bright rose, large, full, and of excellent shape and substance.

Lælia; shaded rose, very large, full, and very fine.

Le Rhone; vermilion, colour rich and brilliant, large, full, and of good form, excellent for masses: one of the best.

Lord Raglan; scarlet crimson, edges violet crimson, large and full.

Lord Macaulay (Wm. Paul); rich scarlet crimson, sometimes maroon crimson, large and full, petals of great substance, good habit, foliage handsome: a first-class Rose.

Madame Alfred de Rougemont; pure white, lightly and delicately shaded with rose and carmine, large and full, shape of the "Cabbage Rose:" one of the best.

Madame Clemence Joigneaux; red, shaded with lilac, large, full, and fine.

Madame Derreux Douvillé; delicate glossy rose, bordered with white, large, full, and of fine form, good habit.

Madame Emile Boyau (Wm. Paul); flowers soft rosy flesh-colour, changing to blush, sufficiently large, perfect in form, constitution hardy, growth moderate, very constant, distinct, and good.

Madame Rousset; beautiful pink, the reverse of the petals silvery, large, full, finely cupped and good habit: one of the best.

Madame Victor Verdier; rich bright rosy cherry-colour, large, full, and fine form, cupped, blooms in clusters.

Maréchal Souchet; beautiful reddish crimson, shaded with dark maroon, very large and full, petals also large, habit good.

Mrs. William Paul; bright violet red, shaded with fiery red, flowers constantly and in clusters, large and full: one of the best.

Paul Delameilleray; fine purplish cerise, very large and full, excellent form.

Pierre Notting; blackish red, shaded with violet, very large and full, form globular, habit good: one of the best.

Princess of Wales (Wm. Paul); vivid crimson, presenting to the eye an unusual body of colour, owing to the thickness of the petals, cupped, large, very double, and remarkably smooth.

Semiramis; clear pink, blush edges, large, full, and of fine globular form: one of the best.

Sénateur Vaisse; bright red, large, and very double, superb.

Victor Verdier; rosy carmine, purplish edges, a large showy free growing Rose, of good quality, and very effective.

BOURBON PERPETUAL.

Catherine Guillot; deep pink, perfect form, one of the best.

Comtesse Barbantanne; flesh colour, large, full, and of fine form, free and good.

Louise Margottin; delicate satin-like Rose, of medium size and exquisite form.

Louise Odier; fine bright rose, full, very free bloomer.

Madame de Stella; bright rose, large, full, and of fine form.

Modéle de Perfection; lively pink, very pretty, blooms freely; one of the best.

BOURBON.

Souvenir de Malmaison; clear flesh colour, edges blush, beautiful, very large and full.

Victor Emanuel; purple and purplish maroon, large and double, good and distinct.

NOISETTE.

Celine Forestier; pale yellow, free bloomer, large and full.

CHINESE.

Mrs. Bosanquet; delicate pale flesh, large and double.

TEA-SCENTED.

Alba Rosea; white, centre rose, large, full, and very sweet.

Comte de Paris; fresh-coloured rose, superb, very large and full.

Countess Ouvaroff; rose, shaded, large and full.

Devoniensis; pale yellow, superb, very large and full.

Enfant de Lyon; pale yellow, large and full.

Gloire de Dijon: yellow, shaded with salmon, very large and full; a superb rose.

Louise de Savoie; fine yellow, large and full.

Madame Damaizin; salmon, large and full, free bloomer, and hardy.

Madame de St. Joseph; salmon pink, beautiful, very large and double, very sweet.

Madame Villermoz; white, centre salmon, large, full, and good.

Marquise de Foucault; white, fawn, and yellow, variable, large and double: one of the best.

Moiret; pale yellow, shaded with fawn and rose, superb, very large and full.

Narcisse; fine pale yellow, large and full.

President; rose, shaded with salmon, very large, and of good form.

Souvenir d' Elise Vardon; creamy white, centre yellowish, very large and full: a splendid rose.

Souvenir d'un Ami; salmon and rose, shaded, large and full, fine.

Some of the varieties above enumerated are very double Roses, and beautiful when forced, although not suited for out-door culture, the buds seldom expanding clean and fully there. The colours of Roses are much altered by forcing, coming much paler, especially if a great degree of heat be maintained. The alteration is least visible in the deep and decided colours.

LATE FLOWERING.

To obtain Roses late in the season, the first point necessary is to keep the plants in a growing state. For this purpose the Autumnals must, of course, be taken; and it has doubtlesss been observed by all Rose-cultivators, that many of these Roses produce flowers at the termination of almost every shoot; or, in other words, *if they grow, they flower.* In the spring of 1843 I shifted about 100 of these, from three-inch into five-inch pots, selecting the freest bloomers, and plunging them, when shifted, in the open ground. Through the early part of summer all the flower-buds were nipped out as soon as seen. Notwithstanding the deprivation of the early blossoms, the plants, by continuing to grow, formed fresh flower-buds. Those formed late in the season were suffered to remain, and in September, *before frost*, the plants were removed to a cold pit, giving all available air by day, and covering with a straw mat by night. They were crowned with flower-buds when placed in the pit; these gradually unfolded, and I cut bunches of Roses at Christmas, in great perfection. It was certainly a mild autumn; and perhaps a more certain method of obtaining success would be, to take the plants at once to the forcing-house, or other greenhouse, where they would probably continue flowering still longer, as the dampness which destroys many of the backward flower-buds in a cold pit might there be prevented.

For this purpose, such kinds as produce a great quantity of flowers, and open freely, should be selected; for instance, Bourbons: Armosa, Queen, and Phœnix—Noisettes: Fellenberg, and Euphrosyne—Chinese: White, Fabvier, Bardon, and the like—are of the best description.

PROPAGATION.

Roses are capable of being increased in a variety of ways. We will follow out their propagation by three methods, which will suffice for our purpose; namely, Grafting, Budding, and Cuttings.

GRAFTING.

Grafting is performed with the greatest success during winter: the end of January, or beginning of February is a very good time. By this method we would propagate the hard-wooded varieties only; the varieties of Rosa Indica being successfully increased by cuttings.

CHOICE OF STOCKS.

Either the Boursault, Manetti, or Dog Rose, may be used as stocks, selected of various sizes, the greater part about the thickness of an ordinary cedar pencil, and potted in three-inch and five-inch pots a twelvemonth before required for grafting.

Having admitted the Manetti in our list of stocks, and knowing the popularity it enjoys at the present moment, it appears desirable to make a few remarks in reference to it. I am quite satisfied that its value is still overrated. A principal objection against it lies in the multitude of shoots it produces. Despite of every effort, the shoots of the budded stock will push into growth, causing a deal of trouble, and, if not closely watched, debilitating or destroying the foreign kind. The statement that many kinds grow more vigorously on this stock than on the Dog Rose is perfectly true; but in reference to the strong growers, is not their growth, when on their own roots, as vigorous as can be matured by our not over sunny autumns? Then the vigour derived by the weak growers is but transitory: it is the result of over-stimulation. The system becomes surcharged with food, hence a reaction: debility ensues, and the whole plant retrogrades. Where, then, are the advantages? The Boursault was said to be the best stock not long ago, but what Rose amateur prefers it now? The Manetti stock has been tried here for several years, and under various modes of treatment; but for the reasons above assigned it is not a general favorite.

SCIONS.

Having our stocks ready, we proceed in search of scions. The hardest, best-ripened wood should be chosen, and cut into lengths of two or three inches. Two, or at the most three buds are sufficient for each scion.

MODES OF GRAFTING.

Wedge-grafting is a favourite method on the Continent, but whip-grafting, and the simplest form of it, is easier of application, and quite as successful. Under this mode, the stock should be cut down as close to the pot as the leaving a smooth portion to graft upon will allow. It is of importance that the stock and scion be of the same size, and each should be cut in an oblique direction, taking care to make the cuts of the same length, and even, that the bark of the scion may fit exactly *upon* the bark of the stock. The two should then be bound firmly together with soft bast, taking care not to displace the scion in the operation.

GRAFTING COMPOSITION.

It is now necessary to exclude air and water, which may be done by melting the following ingredients together over a slow fire, and laying on the composition, while warm, with a flat stick :—

>Five-eighths Black Pitch.
>One-eighth Resin.
>One-eighth Tallow.
>One-eighth Bees' Wax.

This composition becomes hard when cold.

GENERAL TREATMENT OF PLANTS.

The newly-grafted plants should be placed where a steady bottom heat can be maintained. The eyes of the stock will vegetate in abundance, but should be kept in check until the stock and scion are firmly united, and the latter pushed into growth, when they may be entirely eradicated. A shoot from the stock, growing at the place of union, will be very serviceable in drawing the sap upwards to the scion; but it should not be allowed to grow too fast, or it will be at the expense of the latter. When the scions first shoot, it is necessary to pass a mat over the frame or house, to protect them from the sun, or the young and tender leaves will be withered up, and the scions probably perish. When the shoots are two or three inches long, the plants may be removed to a cold pit, where many of them will bloom well the same season: if left to flower in heat they become drawn and weakly, and the flowers thin.

BUDDING.

The operation of budding has been so much written on, and is so generally understood, that it appears quite unnecessary to enter into the details of performance here.

The stocks which are intended to be budded should be potted in the previous autumn, in five-inch and six-inch pots; or they may be budded as they stand in the ground, and potted afterwards early in autumn, while the buds are still in a dormant state. Clean, healthy young stocks should be selected, varying in height from six to eighteen inches; they should be looked over once or twice, to remove any superfluous buds that may push; for two taking an opposite course of growth are sufficient, and by the removal of the supernumerary ones these will grow stronger. In July, or as soon as the bark runs freely, they may be budded, or they may be budded in the main stem if preferred; and about three weeks afterwards the bast, or worsted, should be removed: the buds should not be encouraged to break, or they will probably be injured by the frost in winter. In autumn or spring they may be potted into eight-inch or nine-inch pots, in the compost previously recommended.

MANAGEMENT OF BUDDED PLANTS.

In spring, when the buds have shot a few inches, the growing points should be nipped out, by which means lateral shoots will be formed, the Autumnals flowering freely the same season; many, in fact, almost as well as at any subsequent period. The Summer Roses will not bloom till the following year.

BUDDING TWO KINDS ON ONE STOCK.

If, in budding, we wish to unite two or more kinds on one stock, we should take care that the buds be taken from plants of the same habit and strength of growth. Thus Noisette: Caroline Marniesse (white) and Fellenberg (crimson), would class well together. Bourbon: Madame Angelina (cream) and Souchet (purplish crimson). Tea-scented: Niphetos (lemon) and Bougère (bronze). Chinese: Madame de Rohan (white) and Prince Eugene (crimson-purple); and the like.

CUTTINGS.

Propagation by cuttings may be performed with success all through the growing season. As soon as the forced plants have bloomed, the shoots taken off, when pruning for a second bloom, may be cut to a joint with two or three eyes, allowing the leaves to remain on all excepting the bottom eye intended to be inserted in the soil. About six of these cuttings placed round a four-inch pot, in equal parts of loam, leaf-mould, and sand, will be sufficient. They should be placed firmly in the pots, and afterwards well watered through a fine rose; then plunged where they will have a moderate bottom heat, and be shaded from the mid-day sun. In a few weeks, when rooted, they may be potted separately into three-inch pots, and gradually hardened off. The same soil may be used as before, but broken up fine, or sifted, with the addition of a little sand. Cuttings will strike through the summer, and at any period when the young wood can be obtained well ripened. They may be taken as late as September, but must then remain in the cutting-pots during winter, and be potted off early in spring.

THE AUTOBIOGRAPHY OF A POT-ROSE.*

CHAPTER I.

PROPAGATION—EARLY GROWTH—CHANGE OF HABITATION.

A WRITER of no mean authority has said, that whenever an individual essays to speak of himself, we should listen with attention, as we may almost invariably gather from his remarks an insight into his character and nature. It is because I believe in this opinion that I am about to relate my own history; and if, by withdrawing the veil, the public, knowing more of my nature, should think less favourably of me, I shall at least have the satisfaction of having dissipated a false reverence upheld only by seclusion, and my associates and followers may be gainers by the light of truth thus reflected on my path. Heroes and hero worship! I advance no claim to the former, and am not much enamoured of the latter. If my autobiography, plainly and honestly written, should establish any thing, it will be simply this, *that I was a successful Pot-Rose.*

Much that occurred for the few first weeks of my existence at Pottletown is of course not very vividly before me; and lest I should mislead the public, by stating that

---

* This autobiography, originally written for "The Florist" in 1853, is reproduced here by the request of valued friends.

which is only hearsay, it is perhaps better that such should be passed over in silence. I, however, distinctly remember existing as a short branch, terminated by a flower-bud, in company with other branches, on what is termed the parent tree; and although deriving sustenance from the parent root and through the parent stem, I had a certain sense of my own independence—of my capability of becoming a separate individual, and being in after-times the main stem whence should arise branches like myself. As I heard one and another bestow a passing word of praise on the freshness, beauty, or fragrance of my flower, but reserve the *comble de gloire* for the plant on which I grew, I longed for the time when my master, who was a nurseryman, should see fit to detach me from my parent, and place me in the state of a cutting, to begin life entirely on my own account.

Accordingly, one morning, just as my flower had dropt, I heard with joy, as he gently pressed me between his finger and thumb, that I was "ripe enough," to use his own words, and that on the morrow I was to become a cutting. As the preparation for the coming event was made beneath my own *eyes*, I shall relate, as briefly as possible, the bare facts, not troubling the reader with my hopes, fears, and aspirations, as they may be more easily imagined than described. First of all was brought into the house where I grew about a peck of pure yellow loam, chopped fine, but not sifted; it appeared to have been the top-spit of an old pasture, cut and laid up to dry and air some months previously; the next material was about half a peck of decayed leaves, technically called leaf-mould, and next about a quarter of a peck of white sand. These materials were laid on a flat board and thoroughly mixed together, by turning them frequently with a small spade, and then pronounced ready for use. I now saw a quantity of pots brought in, of the size called large sixties, and a boy followed with some broken pots under his arm, some brickbats, and a hammer. He began breaking the pots into pieces nearly the size of the bottom of the pot, and put one piece the concave side downwards over the hole of each pot; he then broke the bricks into pieces about the size of a nut, put a handful over each piece of crock, and filled the pots with the soil previously prepared, pressing it down rather firmly, and striking it off level with the top of the pot with his hand. I now made a pretty shrewd guess that into one of these pots I was to go; and with an exulting heart (ah! I little knew then what I had to go through before attaining that separate and independent existence I so much longed for,) I saw my master approach with a little white-handled knife in his hand, and before I scarcely knew it, I was severed from the stem. After the *débris* of my flower was cut off, there remained two leaves; the upper one was left intact, and the lower removed; the stem was then cut straight, just below where the bottom leaf joined it, and I was a cutting "made." The accompanying woodcut represents, as nearly as I can remember, my appearance at this early epoch of my career.

I was now inserted, in company with three others, in one of the pots previously described. A hole was made in the soil at the side of the pot with a dibble, about the size of an ordinary cedar pencil, and the lower two-thirds of my length were placed firmly under the soil. The pot was then removed to a frame, with a gentle bottom-heat, and plunged to the rim in sawdust. For the first few days I suffered greatly, owing to my old sources of nourishment being cut off, and having as yet no power of appropriating the new ones at my disposal. I am sure, if my master had not exercised the greatest care and watchfulness over me, I must have died; and I resolved, if I recovered, to show my gratitude, by throwing blossoms and odours around his dwelling all my life. He kept a tank of warm-water flowing beneath me night and day, by which means not only was the soil in which I was

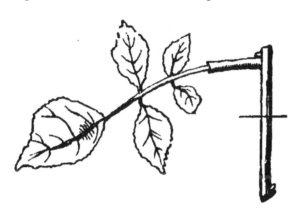

placed made warm and comfortable, but a moisture arose and adhered to the under-sides of my leaf, which proved peculiarly refreshing. Whenever the sun burst upon me, threatening in my then state to exhaust me of my juices, he ran with a mat to afford me shade; and he further refreshed me morning and evening with a dew-like shower, thrown through a fine-rosed syringe. In about eight days the juices exuding from the top and bottom of my stem had formed a callus; and a few days later white porous roots began to form, with sponge-like points, that sucked up the moisture from the soil, and I felt my almost exhausted strength rapidly recruiting. My master now allowed a little sun to fall on my leaf in the morning, and admitted a little air into the frame in which I had been closely shut for a fortnight. By this treatment my strength became so great, and my roots spread so rapidly, that the eye in the axil of my leaf began to grow, and I was shaken out of the cutting-pot and placed in a pot of the same size by myself, in a soil something similar, but with decayed manure instead of leaf-mould, and about one-fourth the quantity of sand. I was here separated from my companions, one of whom had died a cutting, not having been sufficiently ripe when taken; one had not yet rooted, having been too ripe; and the fourth was placed in a separate pot, like myself. I was now carried back to a frame with bottom-heat, syringed with water morning and evening, and shaded from the sun as before. For the first two or three days very little air was admitted; but after that time more and more was given every day, the shade was made lighter by degrees, till at last the frame was entirely removed, and I was exposed to the sun and air night and day. It was now July, and the growing season was before me: my first anxiety was to shew my gratitude to my master, and being of the kind called "autumnal," by the third week of September I produced three, not over large, but finely-shaped and highly-coloured flowers.

As the nursery in which I grew was much visited by lovers of flowers, I heard many high encomiums passed on me; and one evening I was purchased by a country squire, a piece of white paper was tied round my pot, and I was placed inside his carriage; and I, who before had only lived, now lived, and *moved* I knew not whither. It was gratifying to me to see how my new master gazed on me, handled me, and inhaled my attar breath, regarding me, as I thought, with more than usual interest, because he considered my destiny altogether changed in his hands. For my part, I resolved to do my best to please him, as I had done for my former master. Soon the carriage stopped;

I was handed out, passed through the hall and drawing-room, admired by the servants and ladies, and placed by my master in the conservatory. I had not been long here before I saw a red-faced, happy-looking man, without a coat, and with a blue apron, coming towards me with a watering-pot; this, as I afterwards learned was John, the gardener, to whom I took at once, and of whom I shall have more to say by and by. My master met him close by me; and a conversation immediately ensued, ending by John expressing himself highly pleased, but wishing I had been a "wee bit bigger." When I had shed my flowers, I was taken out of doors; and a frosty night having denuded my branches of their leaves, I was removed to a dry cold pit for winter quarters.

CHAPTER II.

GENERAL CULTURE—PRUNING—MANETTI STOCK— PREPARATION FOR FORCING.

THROUGHOUT the winter months I gave very little trouble, although I received every attention that was necessary. The soil about my roots was kept rather dry; sometimes I did not receive any water for a fortnight together, for John the gardener knew well that, as my roots were in an inactive state, such a stimulant would prove injurious rather than beneficial. When the weather was fine, the top of the frame was pulled off, so that I was fully exposed to the sun and air; and, if wet, it was so tilted, that a circulation of air was admitted, though the rain was excluded. When the weather was frosty, the frame was kept closely shut, and sometimes at night a straw mat was drawn over the glass. Thus I passed my first winter, in company with other plants; and when the spring arrived, my powers were so invigorated by the rest I had received, that I felt prepared to grow and blossom with unusual vigour. Early in March I was pruned. I had seven shoots, four strong ones placed at about equal distances, and three weaker ones rising between the former. The latter were cut off close to the main stem, and the remaining four were shortened to two eyes each, so that I might produce eight blooms in June, which were considered a sufficient number for my constitutional strength. A month after this I was placed in a larger pot, of the size called 48, in the same soil as that last used, and plunged on the top of a dung-bed, without any frame. The warmth thus generated about my roots stimulated them to feed and grow, and the increase in the size of my branches was proportionately great. Eight flowers was the number actually produced; and I need not say that I received a liberal supply of weak liquid manure from the commencement of growth till their development.

When the flowers were over, the supply of water was again diminished, which was quite in accordance with my feelings; for after so much exertion I required temporary rest. I remained inactive for about three weeks, when I was again potted into a larger pot, this time No. 24; again freely supplied with water, and stimulated by bottom-heat to a new growth; and I produced in September no less than twenty flowers, which, if of smaller dimensions than those of the summer growth, were pronounced superior in shape and colour. I now saw that my master began to grow proud of me; he brought all his friends to see me, and when he found them interested in my appearance, he gave them my history in brief or detail, according to the humour of the moment. Some I saw smile at the earnestness with which he spoke of various matters; and one young gentleman, a philospher I think they called him, said gravely, shaking his head, that it was monstrous for a reasonable man to occupy himself so earnestly with such trifles; that " the proper study for mankind was man." My master, who was a man of most amiable and even temper, smiled, and calmly replied, that it had never been the business of his life, but only his recreation, and as such it had yielded him an amount of health and calm enjoyment which he would not have exchanged for the purple of an emperor or the riches of the Sacramento. As my master's garden was celebrated for many rare and fine things, it was often the resort of certain *savans* of horticulture. The gardener John was not himself of that class. He was a plain, shrewd, practical man, honest and skilful, not dogged and averse to new things or new schemes because new, but averse to replace old by new before testing the latter by experiment. I often heard some well-fought battles between John and the *savans;* and while the *savans* seemed to know most of theory, it seemed to me that John knew most of practical gardening. Of this I felt sure, after hearing John argue one night with one of these *célèbres*, a General, to whom my master appeared to pay great deference on the subject of Rose-growing. A new stock from Italy was the subject of discussion, I think they called it Manetti. John was told this stock was to surpass all other stocks. When budded on it, Roses were to grow twice as fast as on any other, and never to spawn or sucker; the most shy and delicate were to become free and robust even on the poorest soils; and, in fact, the sooner every other stock was rooted out of the garden and replaced by this, the better. As the General spoke of his own experience, and was wholly disinterested in the matter, my master became a convert. I trembled, when John quietly said, "Let us *try* this stock

first, and if it prove equally good on our soil, we can then replace our other Roses by it." My master seemed to think this course reasonable, and, liking to humour John, adopted it; and that he was well pleased with his decision, the sequel will sufficiently shew.

This has led me to a rather serious digression. To

return. My September flowers had fallen, and I learnt that next year it was the intention to "force me"—that is, to change my seasons, so as to develop my first blossoms in March, instead of June. To this end the pot in which I grew was laid on its side, so that I might get no water naturally or artificially, but sink rapidly into a state of rest. This I did, and was pruned and conveyed to a cold pit, there to wait till the first week of January, which was the commencement of the forcing season. The operation of pruning this year seemed much more difficult than before; I had a great number of branches, some weak and some strong, some well and some ill placed. It was evidently a puzzle even to John what to do for the best; and he walked round me, and looked at me some time before he could make up his mind to begin. At last he seemed to have decided which shoots should remain; and he began removing the others carefully one by one till only twelve were left—one tall shoot in the centre, and the others disposed around it at about equal distances. These shoots were then shortened: on the strong ones were left about five eyes, and on the weak ones two or three, and I was pronounced pruned ready for forcing. My appearance when pruned, at the end of my second year's growth, was something like that represented above.

CHAPTER III.

I AWAKE—TEMPERATURE OF FORCING-HOUSE—GREEN-FLY—MILDEW—I BLOOM—STAND FOR MY PORTRAIT—I BLOOM AGAIN—AM SHIFTED—FUTURE PROSPECTS.

HEIGH-HO! Where am I, and what has been the meaning of so much bustle, of which I have a somewhat indistinct though certain recollection? Ah! now I understand it all. I have been half asleep, and am only awakened to a state of thorough consciousness by the playing of a shower of milk-warm water over my naked branches. It was a frosty morning in January; *my* winter had already passed; I was in the forcing-house; John was using the syringe, and a moist genial warmth rose from the pipes as some few drops of water fell upon them. The wind was blowing keenly from without, and the snow was trying hard to find some crevice through which to enter, as if seeking shelter from the driving blast. But in vain. John held the maxim that "what was worth doing at all was worth doing well;" and he saw with satisfaction from within that he had proved more than a match for frost and snow; they were excluded, and I was safe.

Not to mislead my readers, or lay myself open to a charge of egotism, I may perhaps be allowed to say that I was not alone; my companions were various: there were the bashful Moss, the sturdy Hybrid Chinese, the fragrant Hybrid Perpetual, the clustering Noisette, the ever-blooming Bourbon, and the delicate-coloured Tea-scented, of various shades, all ready to spring into life and beauty; but as it is enough to tell one's own tale, I shall merely relate what pertains to myself. It was still winter

(January) with the Roses out of doors, but spring had commenced with me; the temperature of the forcing-house in which I had been placed was 50° by day and about 40° by night. It was not, however, suffered to remain long at this point: gradually the heat was raised 10°, and the syringe was used every morning, sparingly if the weather was damp, and freely if sunny; and in some rare instances, if the day happened to be calm and genial, a little air was admitted for an hour or so. When my first leaves expanded, I was indulged with a little weak liquid manure, and this was increased in strength and quantity as my leaves grew and multiplied. The house was swept out at least twice a week; for another of John's maxims was, that "cleanliness was next to godliness;" and every thing around me was so neat and comfortable, that I began to think I had arrived at the summit of plant-happiness, when suddenly there came, from where I know not, a minute insect, the colour of my leaf, which caused me great pain and annoyance. At first I looked upon her as a mere visitor, attracted hither by the warmth and comfort of my dwelling, and though it was irritating enough to have her stalking over the still delicate membrane of my leaf, this I might have borne on account of good nature. But, alas! I soon found that not only had she made up her mind to dwell on my leaves, but also to live on my juices! Puncture after puncture was made with rapid succession, and soon a host of young ones rose to join in the attack. A few days only had elapsed since the appearance of the first of this numerous race; but their voracity was so great that my roots could not meet the demand thus made upon them: in vain I twisted my leaves; the more languid the supply the more violently did they suck my juices, and my health began to decline, when one day the door opened, and John, whom I had not seen for some time, came hobbling in with a stick. With a single glance of the eye he saw how the case stood, and forgetting his rheumatism, he dropped his crutch, and hopped out of the house, shouting, "Jacob—green-fly—tobacco!"

Dire was the commotion; for when John spoke he was heeded, and soon a young man entered the house with a pair of bellows and a flower-pot, filled with something from which ascended a great smoke, and as it curled and twisted around my leaves, these miserable marauders gradually relaxed their grasp, and tumbled into the abyss below. Oh, what a relief to me! The next morning I was syringed more freely than before, and the sensation I experienced was more than ever delightful. I cannot say that I liked the tobacco-smoke of the preceding evening, though I heard the young man who was puffing it with the bellows say it would "do me good;" I believe, however, that it did me no harm, and it was a cheap riddance of so dangerous an enemy. All now went on well for a time, when I was subjected to a fresh annoyance. Owing to the damp, cold weather, John could not give me enough of fresh air, and the atmosphere of the house became rather humid. As a consequence, a parasitical plant called mildew fastened on one or two of my young leaves; but he was soon put *hors de combat* by being smothered in sulphur. Again and again did fresh generations of green-fly attempt to gain a footing; but John, who was now well again, and ever on the watch, quickly dispersed them with a few whiffs from his tobacco-pipe. Thus I passed safely through the trying season, and grew and flourished.

March had now arrived; my spring was merging into summer, and I was a pyramidal plant covered with flower-buds, the sepals just parting and showing the brilliant tint between the segments of green. I had before only excited *John's* praise, but now the house resounded with exclamations of delight; and, to speak the truth, I believed every good word that I heard said of me.

I became a great favourite with the young ladies of the establishment, and they one day brought their drawing-master to see me. My beauty and symmetry so delighted

him, that he obtained permission to take my portrait, which he said he would send to the Editor of the *Florist;* and so thoroughly was I impressed with myself at this epoch of my career, that it is a small effort of the memory to reproduce it here. This, then, was my form and stature at this stage of my existence (see p. 69).

But to return. I was again in bud, I blossomed, and my flowers once more strewed the ground. My seed-vessels were cut off, and I was left in the same house, only more air was now admitted. I was watered frequently and fumigated occasionally, as before; the surface of the soil in the pot was sometimes loosened, and I flowered again early in June. My branches were now perfectly ripened, and my pot full of roots; and as my master suggested that I should be exhibited the following year, I was shifted into a larger pot in rich coarse soil. I was now carried out of doors, the pot plunged half its depth in the ground in a situation freely exposed to sun and air, where I grew vigorously, and was ready to lay up for winter by the end of October.

Well-a-day! Few of you young Pot-Roses know or *care*, in the giddy hour of youth, to what summits of greatness you might aspire! Restrain your carelessness. Moderate your gaiety. Think of me. I, an obscure cutting, destined to become an Exhibition-Rose! to bide 'neath gay and party-coloured tents, to blossom in the presence of royalty! Impossible! yet such is *really* the intention. A bright sunny morning gives John an unusual flow of spirits, and I hear him so communicating with himself while sharpening his knife, preparatory to pruning me for the purpose.

CHAPTER IV.

I AM PRUNED FOR EXHIBITION—CONVEYED INTO THE EXHI-
BITION-HOUSE—TIED DOWN—EXCITED TO GROW—TIED OUT
—SHADED—BLOOMED—VISITORS—MANETTI STOCK.

AND John *did* prune me; for he said, as he cut quite half my branches away, and shortened those he left to two or at most three eyes, that I was one of that sort that required close pruning. But when he had finished me, I saw him pass to my neighbour, who was of a looser and more diffuse habit than myself, and with him, after thinning out, he left from four to seven eyes on each shoot. As we both grew and flowered well at the same time, he was no doubt right in thus varying his practice.

No sooner was I pruned, than I was carried with the rest into the exhibition-house, a beautiful new structure reared expressly for our use. There were twenty-four of us, for although only eight were required at the show, I heard John say it was necessary to have a larger number, to make sure of eight being in full bloom on the show-day. In this, Jacob—who in early life had run off to sea, but returned the first convenient opportunity because *he did n't like it*—acquiesced, saying, "It was n't worth while to risk the ship for a ha'porth o' tar." Jacob was always obedient to orders, and had consequently acquired the privilege of expressing his opinions pretty freely. I was not a little proud of this improvement in my position, the house I now inhabited being so much finer than the one in which I had lived the year before. It was a span-roofed house, the faces looking towards the east and west. A double row of hot-water pipes ran all round the interior; the top-lights on one side slid up and down, and all the side-lights were movable, to command a free supply of fresh air.

It was early in December, about a fortnight after I had been pruned and brought into the house, that the first signs of winter appeared: it snowed very hard, and this brought John in-doors, not that he cared for a little rough weather, but that he considered he might, under such circumstances, be more usefully employed within. He had a skein of bast in his hand, and began work by tying a strong ligature of this material beneath the rim of the pot in which I was. He then tied the ends of my strongest shoots, and brought them down from the perpendicular position in which they grew to a horizontal one, fastening the bast to that passed beneath the rim of the pot. Jacob assisted, and when all was finished he said he thought I was pretty well "rigged out." For although he never alluded to his *first and only* sea-voyage, he had thereby added to his vocabulary certain nautical phrases, which he used unconsciously. This operation wrought a curious change throughout my whole system. The sap, which was just rising, and flowing strongly towards the tops of my leading shoots, to the impoverishment of my lower ones, was now more equally distributed, and I felt the benefit of the change. As the winter proved unusually mild, no fire-heat was applied till the last week in February, when it was thought time to begin, in order to bloom me early in May. Hitherto I had received abundance of air and but little water, that I might continue in a state of rest. John came in one morning soon after artificial heat was begun, and wrote up something in the interior of the house, which almost everybody who came in afterwards had the curiosity to read; it was: "N. 45°; D. 55°; Chis., May 8," signifying that the night temperature was to range about 45°, and the day temperature 55°, and that we were to be exhibited at Chiswick on the 8th of May. The former was for the guidance of Jacob, who attended to the fires; the latter for his own, that time might not slip away unnoted. The treatment I henceforth received was almost the same as that of the previous year, only the temperature was some degrees lower. Thus February, March, and the first half of April passed away, and my flower-buds were just showing colour. I had grown remarkably tall and handsome, and become a flourishing young plant. My next neighbour but one was already in bloom; but the others were still, like myself, only children of promise. Such of our master's friends as had seen our progress of late (I can no longer speak of myself as disconnected from my companions) had spread our fame abroad, and it was rumoured that numerous applications would be made to see us. One of John's friends, who had been accustomed to win the gold medal at the exhibition, called about this time, and frankly owned himself beaten, saying, good-humouredly, that he should try hard to recover his position next year. Notwithstanding the excitement arising as the show-day drew near, John " kept the even tenour of his way," knowing well the prize was not his till won. As the buds prepared to expand, he drew a thin canvas shade over the glass, to break the sun's rays, and syringing was now dispensed with.

Time passed on, and it wanted but two days to the show, and it was the last day of receiving company, as my master did not admit visitors to the garden the day before the show, because John was too much occupied in getting us ready to pay them proper attention. I have said it was the last day we were to be seen prior to the show, and the company was thronging to and fro from morning till night. Among others, I was not a little delighted to recognise my old friend the General, who, two years ago, had counselled our destruction in favour of the Manetti. The General was an exact man, and fond of uniformity; he used to prune his own roses, and would cut their heads off right and left, without reference to good practice, in order to keep the whole on a dead level. Oh, how often I had wished that he would come and see us now! Well, he came, and brought his gardener Simon, a young man, with him; and I listened attentively to the conversation that took place, hoping to hear something of my rival. But in vain. John spoke, the General spoke, and Simon spoke, but not a word fell from any of them concerning the Manetti stock. After examining us individually, my master and the General quitted the house, while John and Simon were left standing opposite to me. Each looked significantly at the other for some time without speaking. John, as I afterwards inferred, waiting his opportunity to inquire of Simon the success of the Manetti stock, while Simon was wishing to draw from John the principles of culture by which he had developed such magnificent plants.

Simon at length broke silence, and the following colloquy took place:—

Simon. Wonderful! I couldn't have believed it; though, to be sure, everybody in Cheerup and Pottletown has been talking about 'em for weeks; and Mr. Leek, the nurseryman, said it was a horticultural triumph. They say "it is better to be born lucky than rich;" and you, no doubt, have found out some wonderful manure, or some secret, which you will keep for your own use, and I don't blame you.

John. Stop, stop, my young friend; not so fast: I have no faith in luck, and have no secrets.

Simon. Well, I can't understand it, then. But of course we can't expect you to tell everybody, if you have.

John. Perhaps some people might call it luck, and some might call it a secret; but you see *I have no Roses on Manetti stocks.*

Simon. Oh, pray don't say any thing about that in master's hearing, for he has become almost tired of Rose-growing through the introduction of that abominable thing.

John. How, doesn't it grow well?

Simon. Grow well! Yes, *too* well. It grows *so* well that there is now nothing but itself in the way of Roses left in the garden.

John. But are not the young plants fine?

Simon. Yes, fine the first year, but seldom afterwards. With us, ground-shoots spring up in quicker succession, and ten times more numerous, than from the Dog-Rose; and no amount of watchfulness on my part could prevent the exhaustion and death of the sorts budded on it.

John. The *stock* has been successful then, if the sorts budded on it have failed. But do they not say it is *more excitable* than any other stock, and that Roses break and blossom earlier on it?

Simon. Excitable! Yes. Last spring my Roses broke a fortnight earlier than other people's, and were frosted in consequence, while theirs remained unscathed.

John. Still, as they say it has no thorns, how delightful it must be to be able to bud Roses without pricking one's fingers!

Simon. No thorns, eh! Well, if I was at home my coat would testify the reverse of this, and only look at my torn fingers: why, it is the thorniest of all stocks. But, as we are going to throw them all away, if you would like to try it, I will send you some.

John. Thank you; but I must no longer conceal the truth: I have already tried it. I wanted a confirmation or contradiction of my conclusions, and your opinions are in exact coincidence with my own. It may do well under *special* circumstances, but it is not the stock for *general* use.

Simon. You surprise me! But here is my master; and before leaving, "have you *really* no secrets in growing these Roses?"

John. None but what I am willing to communicate to any one who is willing to listen. Gardening, to be successful, must be a labour of love; and the advancement of it as an art should never be lost sight of.

In continuation, John explained to his young friend how, years ago, he began by reading from the most authentic sources, and worked in with his own ideas what his judgment approved. Thus, aided by close observation, he founded a complete theory on which he built his practice. That practice I have already detailed in this autobiography. "Luck and secrets, young man," added John, "are only idle men's excuses. Knowledge of first principles, experience, care, watchfulness, and labour, are the grounds of success in every branch of culture." Simon departed apparently treasuring in his memory these last words of John, whom he seemed to regard as a Mentor in gardening.

CHAPTER V.

I AM WASHED AND DRESSED FOR THE SHOW—JOURNEY TO CHISWICK—ARRIVAL AND INCIDENTS THEREON—RESULTS OF THE SHOW—COMPANY—MY RETURN—MORE COMPANY AT HOME—THE PHILOSOPHER—STUDY OF MANKIND, AND BUTTERFLIES—CONCLUSION.

EARLY on the morning preceding the show, John and Jacob came in and selected ten of us: I need hardly say that he chose such as were in fullest and finest bloom; and it was highly gratifying to me to find myself one of the first fixed upon. I was carried into the shed to be washed, dressed, and packed; my leaves were sponged, my shoots carefully tied up, and I was then packed in a covered van with my companions, who had been similarly treated, and delivered over to the charge of Jacob, whom John told ten times over to let old Dobbin walk gently, that he might not shake us. Notwithstanding this precaution on the part of John, I found myself, as usual, none the better off for being transferred from his care: Jacob, though clever and attentive, was young, and so elated was he with this his first journey to Chiswick, and the auspicious circumstances attending it, that, unknown to John, he took his cornopæan with him; and no sooner was he clear off than he began to play his favourite village airs. Old Dobbin, who had been a trooper in early life, was soon on his mettle, and *would* prance and caper, despite of Jacob's earnest efforts to restrain him. Fortunately the cessation of the war-notes and a little coaxing brought him to a stand; not, however, till my buds and blossoms had been shaken within a hair's-breadth of snapping. Jacob, pale with fright and hair on end, looked into the van, and pushed his horn under the sawdust in which we stood, apparently thankful that matters were no worse, and the rest of the journey was pursued in ease and safety. On reaching Chiswick, we were carried from the van to the tent on hand-barrows; but, alas! when we arrived there the tables were covered with plants, and we were set on the grass inside the tent. Here we remained about an hour, buffeted by every passer-by: first, a coat-tail swung round and knocked off one of my buds (Jacob remarking that exhibitors in tail-coats should pull them off before walking among exhibition plants, and wishing them *at sea*, the worst wish he was capable of uttering); then a leg brushed me, bruising both leaves and flowers, and I sustained more injury in that short period than during the whole journey from Cheerup to Chiswick. Indeed I never spent so unhappy an hour in my whole life; for, apart from the unpleasantness of my situation, I saw John's long-sustained labour ruthlessly wasted. It seemed there was a dispute about the benches. One of John's competitors had arrived at the show first; and finding John's roses finer than his own, had spread his over a larger surface than usual in order to squeeze John's tight into a corner. But Jacob was not to be out-manœuvred so : he argued, grew angry, and, less wily than his antagonist, visited him with the expressive but disrespectful and impolite term of "dodger," wished him *at sea*, and was preparing to back his arguments by physical force, when John opportunely arrived, and, as usual, brought peace and satisfaction in his train. On understanding the question, he appealed to the fairness of his competitor; but meeting with no response, he went direct to the authorities. The result was, John's argument was pronounced sound and fair, and each had allotted to him his rightful space. But the movement had been artfully contrived, for it left John but half an hour to prepare for the Judges; and had the plants been of nearly equal merit, the loss of time might have been fatal to him. As it was, John won the prize, and the disturber was seen no more that day. I could relate many wise and important things which the Judges said when settling the awards; but as they were said "under the rose," I forbear, sad as the loss may be to the floricultural community. I cannot help saying, however, that one of them, a rough-looking man, said *I* was a "stunner." The company in general admired us very much; and the Prince of gardeners said of me, that I was the finest specimen of a Pot-Rose that he had ever seen. I am again indebted to my friend the drawing-master (who seemed to take an increasing delight in me) for the annexed portrait of me as I appeared at the great Chiswick show (see p. 80).

Yes, reader, this is as I stood in the presence of Royalty, which had quitted its gorgeous palaces and courtly throng to behold and admire the forms and tints of nature's choicest flowers, at once pleasing the eye with their soft and brilliant hues, and delighting the senses with their balmy perfumes. As the day advanced thousands of happy faces passed us by, their attention often diverted by the bands of music stationed in various parts of the garden. The day wore proudly on, the sun was sinking in the horizon, the music ceased, the company retired, and we prepared to return. As we neared home, I found myself subjected to some awkward jerks, arising from sudden stoppages. Poor old Dobbin had found the journey

almost too much for him, and I heard Jacob say he expected every minute to see him "founder." Even cheery words at length failed, and we came to a standstill. In this dilemma, Jacob bethought him of his horn, which he drew from under the sawdust, and played a martial air, which stimulated old Dobbin to renewed efforts. As we entered Cheerup the tune was changed to "See the Conquering Hero comes," and I never could satisfactorily settle in my mind whether by this delicate allusion to *our* victory Jacob meant himself or me. It was now two o'clock in the morning, and sundry heads in nightcaps were suddenly thrust out of up-stairs windows, to be as suddenly withdrawn when the cause was made apparent. The climax was, however, reserved for John's cottage, under whose windows Jacob blew so lustily that he made the very welkin ring, and I thought him lucky in being beyond the district of the metropolitan police. I heard him say, "John did n't like things done by halves, and so he meant to give the old chap a 'good un.'" We reached home in safety, though somewhat dusty, thirsty, and fatigued; and long shall we remember that eventful day. Although somewhat bruised with the journey, more company than ever came to see us, as our fame had risen with our success. Among others, the young philosopher made his appearance. I thought he had grown much older within the last two years, and he seemed more humble and deferential than formerly. He conversed with my master about me with evident interest, and appeared to have gathered some knowledge of my habits and nature. I heard John say, after he had gone, that he had written a book on philosophy, which the world had laughed at; and he had therefore given up the "study of mankind," saying, "they could not understand him," and taken to the study of butterflies! John further remarked, that, according to his judgment, he was incomprehensible to *man*, and he supposed *butterflies* would not be expected to understand him.

I might fill volumes were I to set down all who came to see me and all they said; but I fear that I have already told too long a tale, seeing that it is all about myself. Let me, in conclusion, say a word about my master. His garden was open to the humblest as well as the grandest; and I believe he found one of his chief sources of pleasure in the delight which he thus imparted to his fellow-men. Although the villagers thronged his walks at certain hours, no flower was plucked, no border trampled on, for reproof from all would quickly have visited him who should injure the property or do violence to the feelings of the good squire. His presence was always hailed with delight, whether in urging on the young to engage in rural and athletic sports, in encouraging the advanced to sustain the toils and difficulties of business, or in imparting aid and consolation where age and want had rendered such services necessary. Indeed, his every act was prompted by benevolence and high-mindedness; and his influence was even more remarkable for its kind than for its extent.

John received the gold medal from the London Horticultural Society, and did not forget Jacob's efforts in the struggle; and preparations were presently made to maintain the position so sedulously acquired.

Reader, this has been a true autobiography, and not a

mere creation of fancy: I still exist as an exhibition-rose, and should you wish to see me, you have only to look for me at Kensington among the Pot-Roses at the May exhibition of the present year.

WILLIAM PAUL.

Paul's Nurseries, Waltham Cross, N.

PAUL'S NURSERIES,
WALTHAM CROSS, N.

PRICES OF ROSES OF THE GROWER'S SELECTION.

	£ s. d.	£ s. d.
Standard Roses, fine heads, and clear straight stems, good sorts, well varied . per doz.	0 15 0	to 0 18 0
Ditto ditto per 100	6 0 0	
Standard Roses, ditto ditto, new sorts, per doz.	1 4 0	to 2 2 0
Dwarf Standard, ditto ditto, fine heads and good sorts . . . . per doz.	0 12 0	to 0 18 0
Ditto ditto per 100	4 4 0	to 5 0 0
Ditto ditto ditto new sorts per doz.	1 4 0	to 2 2 0
Dwarfs, summer kinds, in variety . per 100	2 10 0	
Dwarfs, Autumnals ditto . per doz.	0 12 0	to 0 18 0
Ditto ditto per 100	3 15 0	to 5 0 0
Ditto ditto new sorts . . per doz.	1 4 0	to 1 10 0
Climbing Roses, in variety . . . per doz.	0 9 0	to 0 12 0
Ditto ditto per 100	2 10 0	to 3 15 0
Dwarfs, mixed, for borders or shrubberies, per 100	1 10 0	

Dwarfs, for bedding or massing, per dozen or 100 of any one sort at considerably reduced prices.

ROSES IN POTS, READY FOR REMOVAL AT ANY SEASON OF THE YEAR.

	£ s. d.	£ s. d.
Hybrid Perpetuals, in fine variety . per doz.	0 12 0	to 0 18 0
Ditto ditto per 100	5 0 0	
Ditto new sorts . . per doz.	1 4 0	to 1 16 0
Bourbon, in variety, finest sorts . per doz.	0 12 0	to 0 18 0
Chinese or Bengal ditto . per doz.	0 9 0	to 0 12 0
Noisette ditto . per doz.	0 9 0	to 0 18 0
Tea-scented ditto . per doz.	0 12 0	to 0 18 0
Climbing ditto . per doz.	0 12 0	to 0 18 0

EXTRA-SIZED ROSES, grown expressly for forcing or greenhouse culture, established in six-inch pots, 2s. to 3s. 6d. each.

A few SPECIMEN ROSES kept on sale, 5s. to 7s. 6d. each.

NURSERY CATALOGUES.

The following Priced Descriptive Catalogues may be obtained free by post:—

- A. Roses.—New Edition published annually in September.
- B. Evergreens, Conifers, Ornamental Trees and Shrubs, American Plants, and Climbing Plants.
- C. Fruit Trees, including Grape Vines and Strawberries.
- D. Hyacinths, Tulips, Gladioli, &c. New Edition annually in August.
- E. Forest Trees.
- F. New Roses, Geraniums, Hollyhocks, Dahlias, Camellias, Azaleas, &c.
- G. Seeds.—Vegetable, Flower, and Agricultural.

Planting to any extent undertaken by Contract or otherwise.

Experienced Gardeners recommended.

IMPORTANT.—All letters should be addressed WILLIAM PAUL—THE CHRISTIAN NAME IN FULL—WALTHAM CROSS, LONDON, N.

WORKS ON GARDENING,
BY WILLIAM PAUL, F.R.H.S.

The Rose Garden, Second Edition	6s. 6d.
The Rose Annual, 4 Coloured Plates, 1858-59	5s. 0d.
Ditto 4 Ditto 1859-60	5s. 0d.
Ditto 4 Ditto 1860-61	4s. 0d.
Ditto 4 Ditto 1861-62	4s. 0d.
Roses in Pots, Third Edition	2s. 0d.
Morning Rambles in the Rose Gardens of Hertfordshire	1s. 0d.
American Plants, their History and Culture	2s. 6d.
An Hour with the Hollyhock, Second Edition	1s. 0d.
The Handbook of Villa Gardening*	2s. 6d.
Lecture on the Hyacinth, delivered before the Royal Horticultural Society	0s. 6d.

* "Well adapted to the end, being of a plain practical character."—*Spectator.*

"We anticipate it will become, as it deserves, a general authority in suburban cultivation."—*Gardeners' Chronicle.*

"Mr. William Paul's contributions to the Horticultural Literature of the day hold a high position among authoritative works."—*Bell's Weekly Messenger.*

Recently Published, Second Edition, Price 6s. 6d.,

THE ROSE-GARDEN,

BY WILLIAM PAUL, F.R.H.S.

The work is embellished with numerous Wood Engravings.

NOTICES OF THE HORTICULTURAL PRESS.

His instructions are full, and precisely what the Amateur requires.—*Gardeners' Chronicle and Agricultural Gazette.*

The book is executed in a very superior style, with numerous engravings, illustrative of the botany, pruning, and arrangement of the flower in beds, &c. Any Amateur who will procure Paul's "Rose Garden" will make his course clear for the successful cultivation of this beautiful flower, and will soon save all that it costs him in the certainty of his operations, to say nothing of the satisfaction arising from doing things well.—*H. B., in Gardeners' Chronicle.*

We have previously noticed the First Part of Mr. Paul's elegant work on Roses. We can now only repeat our commendation of it, and recommend it to such of our readers as may be Rose-fanciers.—*Gardeners' and Farmers' Journal.*

The "Rose Garden" is not only elegant and useful, but, we may add, an indispensable counsellor and work of reference to all engaged in the cultivation of this popular flower.—*North British Agriculturist and Journal of Horticulture.*

Mr. Paul has not only attended to the amenities of his subject in narrating its history and relating much of the best inspirations of the poets, ancient and modern, in its praise, but has given minute and important details of its cultivation within and without doors. . . . . That he is competent to give such advice, we have only to mention that Mr. Paul is the most successful Rose-grower in England.—*Journal of Agriculture and the Transactions of the Highland and Agricultural Society of Scotland.*

The description of the varieties, each group of which is discussed separately, is given on a very complete and excellent plan.—*Annals of Horticulture.*

The important subject of pruning is handled in a masterly manner. . . . . A book full of most useful information.—*Beck's Florist.*

Given in so plain and understandable a manner, that the merest tyro, by following the directions, may count on success.—*Florists' Journal.*

An extremely useful and instructive book, which ought to be in the hands of every cultivator of Roses.—*Cottage Gardener.*

. . . . We have the authority of a Gardener of long experience to state, that Mr. Paul's book is all that is requisite, &c.—*North of Scotland Gazette.*

London: Kent and Co., 23 Paternoster Row; or from the Author, Waltham Cross, London, N., free, by Post, at the price above quoted.

Made in the USA
Middletown, DE
23 February 2022